When you're in a fierce battle against breast cancer, be on the lookout for people—or pets—through whom God delivers His most heartwarming encouragement. My friend Joni Burchett was in the cancer battle for her life, but God blessed her with His warm, personal touch through the pawprints of her Labrador retriever, Hannah. But this isn't just any "dog story." This is a book filled with courage, yet tenderness; bravery, yet gentleness. I highly recommend *Stay* to anyone who is looking for a fresh and unusual touch from the Lord!

JONI EARECKSON TADA
Founder of Joni and Friends International Disability Center

Dave Burchett has written a truly wonderful book. I don't know when I've shed so many tears, laughed so much, and been moved as deeply. It's not just because I'm a lover of dogs (I am), but because this book is profound, refreshing, biblical, and true. It "smells like Jesus"! Read it and give it to everyone you know. They will rise up and call you blessed.

STEVE BROWN
Founder of Key Life Network

You can count on one opposable thumb how many books hold my interest. But Dave Burchett has written an incredible piece that describes what we've been trying to model to you all about God's grace, His astonishing love, and what life feels like when humans discover who He's remade them to be, even on their worst day. And the pages smell like a freshly cut lawn. I gotta get my master to read this!

BALI LYNCH
John Lynch's golden retriever, who loves to chew on her master's books
The Cure *and* On My Worst Day

Dave Burchett

STAY

*lessons my dogs taught me
about life, loss, and grace*

TYNDALE
MOMENTUM®

The Tyndale nonfiction imprint

Visit Tyndale online at tyndale.com.

Visit Tyndale Momentum online at tyndalemomentum.com.

TYNDALE, Tyndale Momentum, and Tyndale's quill logo are registered trademarks of Tyndale House Publishers. The Tyndale Momentum logo is a trademark of Tyndale House Publishers. Tyndale Momentum is the nonfiction imprint of Tyndale House Publishers, Carol Stream, Illinois.

Stay: Lessons My Dogs Taught Me about Life, Loss, and Grace

Designed by Jacqueline L. Nuñez

Edited by Bonne Steffen

Published in association with Jenni Burke of Illuminate Literary Agency: www.illuminateliterary.com.

For information about special discounts for bulk purchases, please contact Tyndale House Publishers at csresponse@tyndale.com, or call 1-800-323-9400.

Library of Congress Cataloging-in-Publication Data

Burchett, Dave.
    Stay : lessons my dogs taught me about life, loss, and grace / Dave Burchett.
      pages cm
    Includes bibliographical references.
    ISBN 978-1-4143-9793-1 (hc)
    1. Dog owners—Religious life. 2. Dogs—Religious aspects—Christianity. I. Title.
    BV4596.A54B87 2015
    248.4—dc23   2014044568

ISBN 978-1-4964-4301-4 (sc)

Printed in the United States of America

26   25   24   23   22   21   20
7   6   5   4   3   2   1

Dedication

The greatest legacy one can pass on to one's children and grand-children is not money or other material things accumulated in one's life, but rather a legacy of character and faith.

BILLY GRAHAM

To my precious grandchildren, Ethan, Clara, and Bennett. Nothing makes me want to finish strong as a Christian, husband, father, and grandfather more than looking into your innocent and loving eyes. I hope that I can teach each one of you the lessons out-lined in this book. But if I am not given that privilege, I wanted you to know that Papa eventually began to figure out what it means to follow Jesus. I love you all dearly and unconditionally.

In His Amazing Grace,

PAPA

Contents

Foreword

WHEN MY FRIEND Rusty Kennedy said I had to meet Dave Burchett, his name seemed vaguely familiar. I realized the familiarity came from years of watching my beloved Texas Rangers on television. Dave's name was often mentioned with various levels of respect by the announcers in the broadcast booth. He is the behind-the-scenes director in the production truck and has been for three decades. I had heard his name countless times in that context. But that was not the reason Rusty suggested we meet.

He told me Dave had written a book about his grace epiphany and journey to freedom in Christ. I read *When Bad Christians Happen to Good People* and was blown away by Dave's honest portrayal of his struggle with performance-based faith. God used that book and others as I pieced together my own discovery of grace and identity that led to MercyMe's album *Welcome to the New*.

So I met Dave and found out he is a lover of grace and baseball and dogs. Is there a better résumé than that? I was touched, challenged, and amazed at the insights Dave has gleaned from his rescued dogs, Hannah and Maggie. I can relate completely to his stories about loyalty, faithfulness, and grace demonstrated by his four-legged friends. We are learning similar lessons of friendship and unconditional love from our own Shetland pony–sized puppy named Lulu.

Just like me (and you), Lulu is a mess, but we love her dearly. What an example of how our heavenly Father looks at the mess we bring to Him yet still loves us with scandalous abandon because of Christ.

There is a grace revival sweeping our land. This delightful collection of lessons will show you how Jesus came to give us a new identity and a way to actually deal with sin. You will see how God can even use rescued dogs to teach a willing student that we don't need to strive to accomplish what Jesus has already done. It's an enjoyable journey of grace with Dave and his four-legged mentors. And I would be remiss if I did not let you know that Lulu gives *Stay* her highest rating of Four Paws.

Bart Millard

Introduction

The one absolutely unselfish friend that man can have in
this selfish world, the one that never deserts him, the one
that never proves ungrateful or treacherous, is his dog.

–Senator George Graham Vest, 1870

I NEVER DREAMED I would write a book about a dog. Granted, I thought my Labrador buddy, Hannah, was pretty amazing. But the idea of a book about her was not even on my radar until a devastating cancer diagnosis threatened to take her away too soon. I began to process the all-too-real possibility that my canine friend would be with us for only a few more days or, if we were fortunate, several more weeks. During those moments of sadness, I decided to journal what I was learning from this special relationship with Hannah, celebrating the memories my best dog friend helped create and the lessons she taught me.

As I prepared for the inevitable loss of Hannah, I learned an eye-opening truth: preparing for death is preparing for life. God has revealed so much to me through this unique canine friendship. God can teach us in many ways; all He really needs is an attentive listener.

I'm reminded of a verse in the book of Job. Job, who had lost everything he held dear on earth, was being counseled by his "friends," who wondered what sin Job had committed to bring about such suffering on one individual. In frustration, Job declared that he could learn more about God and His purpose from His creation than from His people. "Just ask the animals, and they will teach you. Ask the birds of the sky, and they will tell you" (Job 12:7).

It is a sentiment I have often shared.

To be honest, I did not run to Hannah and ask her to teach me. Even I am not that weird. I had no idea how much I could learn when I opened my eyes and heart to what Hannah and her canine compadres have revealed about friendship, loyalty, trust, and grace. I began my dog "training" lessons with an unflappable four-legged instructor. When I started to "get" it, I chuckled at God's sense of humor and, simultaneously, I was touched by His amazing grace. I believe He knew from the beginning of time that I would have this special relationship with Hannah. I believe He knew that I would be fully attentive and engaged after Hannah's deadly diagnosis. God knows how tough it is to get an ADD guy's full attention, so He was not going to waste any chances.

My journey of discovery with dog friend Hannah has been a revelation. Who knew that some of my most significant spiritual growth would come thanks to a rescued puppy? I am not embarrassed to admit that I was discipled by my dog. Author Corey Ford wryly notes that "properly trained, a man can be dog's best friend." I was blessed with an excellent trainer.

CHAPTER I

PUPPY LOVE

There is no psychiatrist in the world like a puppy licking your face.

~ BEN WILLIAMS

My wife, Joni, and I are dog lovers. I grew up with a rescued mutt named Penny. She resembled some sort of mad scientist's terrier creation, and she was my best friend from elementary school until college. Here I am (pictured on the left) with Penny.

Joni loved and grew up in south Florida with a sweet Boxer named Dutchess. Joni and Dutchess made life miserable for the local duck population by chasing them every day.

Dogs have always been a part of our lives. As 2002 approached, Joni and I were at that tough crossroads for every dog owner, facing the decision about what to do when a dog is near the end of its journey. Charlie, our nearly fourteen-year-old golden retriever, was fast approaching that moment. The winter of 2001, he teetered on barely functioning hips which made walking painful.

He was a far cry from the Charlie-is-a-handful years, which is a very kind way of saying he was crazy. Charlie was the perfect blend of alpha-dog testosterone and faithful friend for a household with three rambunctious boys. He ran, chased, wrestled, swam, dived, and cuddled with our sons Matt, Scott, and Brett. Charlie was their buddy through puberty and high school frustrations, much as Penny had served that role with me.

Other than breed differences, there was one other huge difference between Penny and Charlie. Remember Marley, the yellow Lab of book and movie fame, who was described as the world's worst dog? Well, Charlie certainly had to be in the conversation at eighty pounds of hard-charging destruction.

Charlie was particularly psychotic during thunderstorms, causing hundreds of dollars of damage to our home. If a storm hit while we were away, we entered the house with fear and trembling upon returning, afraid to see what Charlie had wrought. One time he chewed off a cabinet door in order to wedge himself under the sink. While he was hidden, he chewed off the sink trap, just to keep his mind off of the booms of the raging storm.

Another memorable time, we discovered our guinea pig's cage ripped apart and its former inhabitant, Squeakers, ominously missing. We feared the worst but found no *CSI: Rodent Edition* evidence of foul play. After a few hours we heard Squeakers's terrified call from underneath a built-in cabinet. Somehow Squeakers had squeezed her brown, black, and white fur-covered frame through a narrow opening to escape thunder-crazed Charlie. No amount of coaxing or food could get that trembling critter to come out of her refuge. She was too far back to reach in and pull her out. Finally, we hired a carpenter to saw a hole in the bottom of the cabinet so Squeakers could be saved.

Then there was the security breach incident. We were away from home when I received a surprise phone call from our security company that an alarm had been triggered. I was worried about the house but also wondered, *Is Charlie okay?* The local police showed up and reported seeing only a tail-wagging and very happy-to-see-anyone golden retriever who, upon further investigation, turned out to be the perp in the caper. In another fit of storm jitters, he had chewed through some wires.

I think you get the picture: Charlie did not handle life's storms well.

Still, in that odd paradigm that only dog people understand, we loved him dearly.

Matt and Scott were off to Baylor University at this time and youngest son, Brett, was just a couple of years away from leaving the nest. With Charlie's failing health, we wondered what our lives would look like without a dog around the house. Should we even consider the scenario of another dog? Perhaps it would be a welcome respite, not worrying about boarding a pet when we traveled or to be able to go out without concerns about what might await us when we got home.

That January, Scott called from school and got right to the point. His girlfriend (now his wife), Caroline, had "inherited" a Labrador puppy that had been passed around the dorm to several foster volunteers. The fun of having a cute puppy on campus had turned into a time-consuming reality: caring for a puppy is not far removed from caring for a baby. Knowing Charlie's condition, Scott and Caroline proposed that Joni and I take her—for a while. Scott hit the most vulnerable and by far weakest link in the family line of canine defense.

Me.

"Caroline has adopted this puppy temporarily. Her name is Hannah. We can't watch her this weekend. Could you keep her until we can find her a home?"

Within minutes of Hannah's arrival at our house, it was obvious that this puppy was going nowhere. She wasn't an ordinary Lab; her coat's color was not the usual light yellow Lab hue. She was a Fox Red Labrador, with the darker reddish tint. They are generally pricey little pups so, in retrospect, it was an added bonus to acquire her for free.

Over the next few weeks, it was clear that this puppy was something special. She had eyes that seemed to look into your soul. Her friendly expression was true to her character and she was more than happy to accommodate anyone who wanted to play at any time. Her ears were as soft as mink. Hannah was a keeper.

From the beginning, she instinctively knew that Charlie could not handle the aggressive play of a puppy. They became instant friends and Hannah was gentle with old guy Charlie in his final days.

I am a TV sports director for the Texas Rangers, which means I am on the road for about half of the baseball season from April through September. In April, I was in New York, working at Yankee Stadium, when Joni called with trembling voice to say she was taking Charlie to the vet for the last visit. He could no longer walk and refused to eat. His once unstoppable body was failing. It was time to say good-bye.

After I hung up, I saw a New York cop outside the stadium with his Labrador police dog at his side. Seeing that sweet Lab hit me hard; I was already missing my crazy friend Charlie. I approached the officer and asked him if I could pet the dog.

"He's working," the officer snapped at me.

"I understand, sir. I was just feeling sad. We had to say good-bye to our fourteen-year-old golden retriever today."

The cop's face immediately softened as he looked at me. "Pet the dog."

"It's okay, officer. I understand that the dog is . . ."

"PET THE DOG."

"Yes, sir."

The power of this unique relationship we forge with our dogs is truly universal.

We had said good-bye to a dear friend. But God had given us a special gift named Hannah.

CHAPTER 2

ALWAYS THERE

It doesn't matter where you are in life . . . just who is by your side.

~AUTHOR UNKNOWN

JOURNAL ENTRY

*Until Hannah came along, I guess I would have said
that my dog Penny was the best canine friend I had ever
had. Don't get me wrong—I loved crazy Charlie. At the
risk of sounding like a bad Julio Iglesias parody, I have
a special place for all the dogs I've loved before. But
Hannah is just so much fun.*

Hannah's athletic feats are a delight to behold. Maybe
it's being around sports for as long as I have that makes me
enjoy them so much. She can focus on a tennis ball and
catch it with more concentration than some outfielders I
have covered in big league baseball (names withheld out of

abundant grace). She is ultracompetitive but never in the ugly way that some bipeds display. As physical as she likes to play, Hannah is also gentle. I can't recall ever getting scratched or nipped by her. She simply plays with doggie abandon that is contagious.

She figured out on her own how to fit three tennis balls in her mouth at once and then spit them in your direction like Snoopy playing shortstop in a *Peanuts* comic strip. That is a gift.

But there is something more than her mad skills that makes Hannah different. Hannah feels like a canine soul mate that arrived at just the right time to walk with Joni and me during our most difficult season, kicked off on March 20, 2006.

We referred to it as D-Day or "diagnosis day" in our marriage. Not surprisingly, I was on the road when I got a voice mail message from my bride. For several months she had some suspicions about a lump in her breast, but she had been faithfully undergoing regular mammograms and exams that had always come back clear. Joni sought a second opinion and a biopsy was ordered. We had been through this before and the results had always been benign. We were unprepared for the news she received that early spring day.

Joni's phone message was a single sentence. Most of life's conversational sentences are blissfully mundane. Things like, "I can't find my keys," "Take out the garbage," or "Please feed the dog." But sometimes a single sentence will change your life. Joni dropped one of those sentences on me: "My spot was cancerous."

That was all she could get out. As soon as I was free, I called her to talk and pray, making arrangements to scurry home. I went with Joni to the appointment with her surgeon, where we received an optimistic initial briefing. A couple of days later the pathology report told another story; we were rocked by what it contained. The tumor was small but very aggressive. A new drug targeted Joni's specific diagnosis of HER2-positive, but if that drug could not be tolerated, the outcome could be far less favorable. Overall the prognosis was optimistic but the journey would be really difficult. I now understood what noted scholar and philosopher Mike Tyson meant when he said, "Everyone has a game plan until they get hit in the mouth." That was how I felt after talking and crying with my wife. After lumpectomy surgery to remove the tumor, we were looking at a year of chemotherapy followed by radiation treatments.

Joni was understandably scared as she set out on this tough journey. At the same time, she fully trusted God for what lay ahead. As we prayed about her upcoming surgery, my beautiful wife dropped another sentence on me that was a game changer.

"Dear God . . . I am not, and I will not, question you."

How can you not want to go into battle with a woman like that? When she got the diagnosis, I told her that I wished I was going through this and not her. She said that she was glad it was her and not me. The miracle of two becoming one is that we both meant what we said.

In the midst of that storm, Hannah nuzzled her way into our fears as a comforting and caring friend. Hannah would be at Joni's side every waking minute when I was gone. If Joni crawled into bed after her treatments, Hannah would stretch out on the floor next to her. That would seem like no big deal, except Hannah normally slept on my side. She changed her treasured routine to be near her friend.

When Joni was feeling better, she would relax in the recliner with Hannah nestled next to her chair, staying there as long as my wife needed to pet the ears of our therapy dog.

When Joni got tired, Hannah would crawl underneath the recliner lift, just to be close. More than once, Joni almost lowered the mechanism on her sleeping friend. Hannah did not bring her toys to Joni when she was sick. The play could wait. She knew what Joni needed in that moment. Her friend needed nuzzles and soft ears to rub.

Hannah seemed to intuitively know what to do to cheer us up, and her eyes communicated what she could not speak. Our human friends did not always do as well.

For example, Hannah never tried to "prepare" us for troubles ahead with stories of other cancer patients. Those who tried to help by recounting stories of terrible side effects and problems were far from helpful. The doctor gave us a good rundown of those possibilities based on Joni's unique circumstances. We did not need random horror stories that might have no correlation to her situation.

Nor did Hannah predict the outcome with phrases like, "You are going to be fine." No one could be completely certain how things would turn out. What we were sure of was that God would be faithful to us each step of the way.

Hannah did not bark in mournful and sad tones or act weird when Joni was around. She was just herself, which was comforting for Joni and for me. Many well-meaning people get weird around sickness.

Hannah's sweet concern for both of us was perfect. So many Christians feel the pressure to say something profound or theologically brilliant. Simple phrases like "I am praying" and "I am here if you need me" pack more punch than a theological dissertation on suffering. Some don't know what to say and then proceed to say it in great detail. Joni and I didn't need to figure this out in the middle of the battle. We just needed to walk with the Lord one step at a time. We knew He had a plan. We were not necessarily convinced that He had told other folks what that plan was.

One of the things Joni and I often heard confessed from people who heard her story was how they wouldn't have been able to deal with adversity as well as Joni handled it. They would. Part of being a follower of Christ is knowing He is with you in times like this. You are given strength and comfort that are supernatural. They are there when you need them. You can't store them for future troubles or put them in a take-out box for later. God apportions that strength and comfort as needed. God's strength for the trial was like the manna provided to the Israelites described in Exodus. You can only partake of the provision for that day. No leftovers allowed.

As Joni wrapped up her treatments, she decided to celebrate surviving the ordeal by taking part in the Susan G. Komen 3-Day, an event that millions of people have experienced in cities across America since it began in 2003. Participants walk sixty miles over three long days. Just over a year after diagnosis day, my bride started training for the walk in Dallas.

Although I wouldn't be able to take each step with her during the event, I trained with her, with daily walks together and longer walks on the weekends when I was home. Hannah was a willing partner in the training walks as well.

When the day arrived, Joni's sister, Gayla, flew in from Florida to join her. Along the way, friends and family stationed themselves at various checkpoints to cheer on and encourage Joni, Gayla, and the countless walkers.

They did the first leg on Friday, and we decided to meet Joni with one of her biggest supporters on Saturday. However, we couldn't just bring Hannah to the event without fanfare. We had to dress her up for the occasion. I found a sassy little pink number at the local pet store and we created a sign. Miss Hannah was none too happy as I wrestled her into her outfit for the day. It was one of the few times I can remember that she truly looked disappointed in me. She squirmed and showed as much displeasure as she could muster with her sweet personality.

Her face couldn't hide her embarrassment as we loaded up to meet Joni and Gayla at one of the checkpoints. But when Hannah saw her human mom and all those people, her demeanor changed completely. The dog smile never left her face. (Hannah's stylish look is pictured on page 9.)

The next day when I pulled out that dreaded stretch outfit, Hannah's attitude did a complete turnaround. She was excited to put on that constricting attire because it meant seeing Mom and new friends!

Our family is grateful for what Hannah gave us during that difficult season. Five years later, she would need the same care and comfort from us.

CHAPTER 3

BE PRESENT

*Dogs . . . do not ruin their sleep worrying about how to keep the
objects they have, and to obtain the objects they have not. There is
nothing of value I have to bequeath except my love and my faith.*

~EUGENE O'NEILL, FROM HIS DALMATIAN, BLEMIE'S,
LAST WILL AND TESTAMENT

JOURNAL ENTRY

One reason Hannah is such a special friend is that she entered our lives during a difficult season when her human mom—my wife, Joni—was diagnosed with breast cancer. Hannah provided a comforting presence during a scary time. I found an anonymous quote that sums up one big reason why: "One reason a dog can be such a comfort when you're feeling blue is that she doesn't try to find out why."

Hannah knew how to deal with people going through an emotionally and physically draining valley. Her solution was simple but powerful.

Be present.

It was just the unsolicited encouragement that Joni and I so needed at the time. When this cancer journey began, we learned a lot of hard lessons. One of the hardest to swallow was people's reactions, how those close to us dealt with tragedy and illness. We had expectations of who would be there for us during the storm, but those expectations were rarely correct. Some people that we were sure would be steadfast became invisible. Others who we would have wagered the mortgage on to be constant encouragers became awkward and distant. When your expectations are met with inconsistent responses from friends and family, it can devastate your spirit and lead to despair.

Although reasons were never given, I could guess why people struggled with our situation, based on the unique baggage they brought to their own story. Perhaps cancer made them fear their own mortality. Some acted as if cancer is contagious. Perhaps they worried they might say the wrong thing. Others might have felt pressure to make sense of a senseless situation or the need to figure out the spiritual reason for the trial, and when they had no answer to give us, they retreated. I understand all that now, but at the time it hurt.

That's what Hannah sensed. Her intuitive evaluation of my emotions was uncanny. Hannah would come to me and nudge me as if to say, "I'm here." As she shifted her big brown eyes toward mine, her gaze communicated, "I don't know how to help, but I wish I could."

There was incredible comfort in her presence.

She was right. That was *all I needed*—presence. When Joni was sick with cancer, all we needed from friends and fellow followers of Jesus was caring presence.

The theology of why bad things happen could wait. The

go-to verse that "all things work together for good" (Romans 8:28, KJV) could be explored when time gave perspective. You don't need to explain or spiritualize trials. You need to be present and willing to walk with your friend or loved one in grace and love. Simple, yet incredibly powerful.

Remember me mentioning Job and his suffering in the introduction? At first, Job's friends were fantastic empathizers. When they simply sat with Job and grieved with him, I am sure he took comfort in these men who cared enough to be present. But then they decided to speak their piece. They resorted to the familiar default mode of needing to "figure out" what Job did to trigger his suffering. They tried to explain what they could not understand.

We had a few "Job friends" in our cancer journey. God was faithful to provide caring people to walk with Joni and me. We thanked Him for those He prompted to love us, instead of wondering why others were not there. That was a spiritual turning point for us.

During Joni's cancer, Hannah obviously had no idea why we were sad. She had no more understanding of Joni's disease than she would later have of her own prognosis. But she could sense our sorrow and she was present in the moment.

Joni's breast cancer treatment included surgery and a year of chemotherapy followed by weeks of radiation. We joked about our weekly dates at the "Slow-Drip Spa," but there was not much humor to be found in the aftermath of those sessions. Joni fought nausea and her plummeting white blood cell counts were dangerously low, compromising her recovery. One day after we returned home from Joni's chemotherapy session, she went straight to the bedroom, exhausted, to try to sleep off the nausea. I sat on the couch in our living room staring at nothing as I tried to process all that Joni was going through.

Hannah sensed my sadness but wasn't sure what to do. She walked by, looked at me, picked up a tennis ball, and brought it to me. I could see a hint of uncertainty in her eyes. I imagined a thought bubble appearing over her head with the message, "Would this help make you less sad?"

I tossed the ball to her, but she did not play with the normal zeal that she had during our games of catch.

This day Hannah caught the ball, calmly brought it back, and gently dropped it in my lap. It was as if she was doing this for me and not her. She was giving me a few moments of respite from my fears. I don't recall another time that she played in that way.

A recent study done by Goldsmiths College in London suggests that dogs may respond more to our emotions than any other species, including our own. According to the study conducted by Dr. Deborah Custance and Jennifer Mayer, dogs will even approach strangers to comfort them, regardless of expectation of reward or care. That certainly makes them different from many humans.

The researchers did the following experiment.

Eighteen pet dogs, spanning a range of ages and breeds, were exposed to four separate 20-second experimental conditions in which either the dog's owner or an unfamiliar person pretended to cry, hummed in an odd manner, or carried out a casual conversation. The dogs demonstrated behaviours consistent with an expression of empathic concern. Significantly more dogs looked at, approached and touched the humans as they were crying as opposed to humming, and no dogs responded during talking.

Humming was included because it is an unusual sound that might arouse the curiosity of the dogs. But interestingly enough, the dogs consistently reacted to the person who was crying instead of the ones humming or talking, regardless of whether the person crying was a dog's owner or a complete stranger.

Jennifer Mayer summed up the surprising result, which was amazing to me.

> If the dogs' approaches during the crying condition were motivated by self-oriented comfort-seeking, they would be more likely to approach their usual source of comfort, their owner, rather than the stranger. No such preference was found. The dogs approached whoever was crying regardless of their identity. Thus they were responding to the person's emotion, not their own needs, which is suggestive of empathic-like comfort-offering behaviour.[1]

The researchers suggested that centuries of breeding had created this type of response in our canine companions. Perhaps. But I align more with Martin Luther's thoughts on this issue: "The dog is the most faithful of animals and would be much esteemed were it not so common. Our Lord God has made his greatest gifts the commonest."

I think God has given us a model of walking, breathing grace in these amazing creatures.

The empathetic instinct to pain that my friend Hannah possesses can be a template for how I can be present with God. There are times when my baggage or fear causes me to be awkward and distant from God. I am not sure what to say or even if God wants to deal with my weak faith again. I am tempted to talk bravely as if nothing is wrong. But my heart is crying out in pain. God comforts me in the brave talking, but He rushes toward the crying of my soul. I think that is what the apostle Paul is describing in Romans, assuring us that the Holy Spirit intercedes on our behalf when we are too anguished to even find words:

> The Holy Spirit helps us in our weakness. For example, we don't know what God wants us to pray for. But the Holy Spirit prays for us with groanings that cannot be expressed in words. And the Father who knows all hearts knows what the Spirit is saying, for the Spirit pleads for us believers in harmony with God's own will.
> ROMANS 8:26-27

The Holy Spirit senses our hearts and literally interprets our anguish to the Father. God desires that we simply be present with Him. We don't need to pray eloquent psalms of petition. We simply put our heads in the lap of Abba Father and say, "I'm here." And isn't it interesting that it is in this very intimate context of submission and tender dependence on the Holy Spirit that the oft-quoted phrase about how "all things work together for good" occurs?

> The Holy Spirit helps us in our weakness. For example, we don't know what God wants us to pray for. But the Holy Spirit prays for us with groanings that cannot be expressed in words. And the Father who knows all hearts knows what the Spirit is saying, for the Spirit pleads for us believers in harmony with God's own will. And we know that *God causes everything to work together for the good* of those who

love God and are called according to his purpose
for them.
ROMANS 8:26-28, EMPHASIS ADDED

We isolate the verse about "everything working for good"
from its context and throw it out as "comfort" for those who
are suffering. Paul says that God is with us in our suffering,
not just for one specific event, but for *all of the trials* we will
face in our lives. All of them will be ultimately redeemed for
those who love God.

The purpose of our trials is not necessarily to have things
work out neatly, according to our desires. Romans 8:29 says,
"God knew his people in advance, and he chose them to become
like his Son." God chose believers to become like His Son. All
of these trials together will cause us to become more like Jesus.
That may or may not mean a particular event will work out
well. How often have we wounded a hurting soul with our shallow spiritualizing when he or she just needed a friend?

Learning to be present for a friend or a loved one is a precious skill. Henri Nouwen captures this heart of friendship well.

When we honestly ask ourselves which persons in
our lives mean the most to us, we often find that it is
those who, instead of giving much advice, solutions,
or cures, have chosen rather to share our pain and
touch our wounds with a gentle and tender hand.
The friend who can be silent with us in a moment
of despair or confusion, who can stay with us in an
hour of grief and bereavement, who can tolerate
not-knowing, not-curing, not-healing and face with
us the reality of our powerlessness, that is the friend
who cares.[2]

It starts with being present, a lesson well taught by my friend Hannah. She gave me a clear example of being present when your friend is hurting. Just be present. Not all-knowing. Not awkwardly fumbling for words. Simply present.

Tonight I got into bed late, and Hannah got up from her comfy bed and walked to my side. Maybe she needed my presence. Maybe she sensed my need for a therapeutic ear scratch. I suspect the truth is that both of us had needs that were met by that simple action of presence and affection. That is how it works when we drop our fears and selfishness to make ourselves lovingly present in a loved one's pain. It is therapeutic for everyone involved.

During Joni's difficult cancer trial we learned that the peace that surpasses all understanding is real. We lived it and we got through a very trying year by leaning on each other, great doctors, good friends, God's grace, and lots of Hannah nuzzles.

CHAPTER 4

LIVE IN THE MOMENT

We never really own a dog as much as he owns us.

~GENE HILL

Journal Entry

You never know when life is going to blindside you. You rock along in the daily routine and expect lights to turn green and skies to be blue. Jesus knows you don't become more like Him when life is all good. I have been on this journey long enough to know that is true. But I still think it would be nice to get a little heads-up before you get sacked.

I learned one of my most valuable lessons from Hannah in the midst of one of our saddest weeks together. I had just stumbled through the back door from an all-night flight in the spring of 2011 when I noticed something was amiss with

Hannah. Normally she would celebrate my arrival with a wild, exuberant, spinning dance accompanied by a vibrating, thumping tail. This time, her greeting was subdued, her gait slow, and her soulful eyes dull.

Joni and I immediately knew that something was wrong. This was not Hannah. Joni wondered if part of a rawhide chew stick that Hannah had devoured the day before was causing an obstruction. "Maybe she got into something outside that upset her tummy," I said hopefully. But we were both fearful that it was something much more serious. Even though she seemed slightly better as the day wore on, we made an appointment with the vet just to make sure.

The news that we received on Friday afternoon, May 6, was much worse than we expected. A suspicious growth on her spleen and fluid in her stomach signaled a grim prognosis. On Monday morning, we went to a specialist who confirmed the diagnosis. Dr. Carmenn Woolley explained the sad options we faced. Hannah had a splenic tumor which, given her age, would likely be malignant.

Our choices were less than optimal. Without surgery, Hannah's tumor would rupture and bleed out and she would likely die within days or even sooner. With the surgery, she would still face an uncertain future, especially if the tumor was malignant. We could be talking a matter of weeks. The surgery was very expensive with no guarantees.

Still, a recent tax refund had given us the rare luxury of money to spend as we wished. Joni had a list of projects far more extensive than the refund would cover, and she had been trying to decide which project topped the list. That night we discussed the new reality. We could just try to keep our canine friend comfortable, or we could use the refund for Hannah's surgery and give her a fighting chance.

Two days later, I picked her up from the Lake Ray Hubbard Emergency Pet Care Center after a successful surgery. So much for the new furniture, house painting, or landscaping. In place of those things, we got a dog friend with a twelve-inch incision on her belly and the hope of some sweet time to say good-bye.

Even after surgery, Hannah's diagnosis was ominous. Splenic hemangiosarcoma. It was a horrible-sounding disease with an even worse prognosis. Without chemotherapy, the survival predictions were nineteen to sixty days. Six months would be a miracle. Dr. Woolley showed great compassion as tears welled in my eyes and spilled down my cheeks. The doctor's eyes grew misty as she shared one of the most painful duties of her job. She handed me a tissue, put her hand on my arm, and quietly said something. Since I was still reeling from the shock of everything that had happened so quickly, her words didn't sink in until later.

"Hannah does not know she is sick. Dogs have no fear of death, so they live in the moment. Enjoy each moment that you have."

I thought about that comment a lot in the days to come. Hannah indeed lived in the moment: she could have any and all treats, she was allowed to sniff a little longer at points of interest during our daily walk, and the tennis ball was tossed in the pool for her an extra time or two before we would head inside.

We marveled at how well Hannah did week after week, often having to remind ourselves that she was sick. We wondered at times if the diagnosis was even correct.

Dogs have no fear of death, so they live in the moment. Isn't that a blueprint for how followers of Christ should live on a daily basis? I had been a Christian for more than thirty years and had not figured out such a succinct philosophy of living. Satan wants us to live in regret of the past and fear of the future, preventing us from contentment in the moment with our God and with those we love.

I began to learn that part of being content on the journey with Jesus is simply trusting Him one day at a time. You can't live in regret of the past. It is forgiven. You can't live in fear of the future. It is in God's hands. Without regret or fear you are free to live in the moment. Or as C. S. Lewis put it, "Where, except in the present, can the Eternal be met?"[1]

Jesus proclaimed that exact message in the Gospel of Matthew.

> That is why I tell you not to worry about everyday life—whether you have enough food and drink, or enough clothes to wear. Isn't life more than food, and your body more than clothing? Look at the birds. They don't plant or harvest or store food in barns, for your heavenly Father feeds them. And aren't you far more valuable to him than they are? *Can all your worries add a single moment to your life?*
> MATTHEW 6:25-27, EMPHASIS ADDED

It was true. Worrying would not add a single moment to my life or to the life of my friend Hannah. Thanks to a kind and wise veterinarian I experienced a spiritual epiphany. If the Bible is true, then the Author of this message is trustworthy. Jesus continued to teach His early followers (and a suddenly focused me).

> So don't worry about these things, saying, "What will we eat? What will we drink? What will we wear?" These

things dominate the thoughts of unbelievers, but your heavenly Father already knows all your needs. Seek the Kingdom of God above all else, and live righteously, and he will give you everything you need. So don't worry about tomorrow, for tomorrow will bring its own worries. Today's trouble is enough for today.

MATTHEW 6:31-34

That was the game plan that I adopted for what I anticipated would be my last summer with Hannah. Live in the moment, seek the Kingdom of God above all else, and the rest will take care of itself. I have to confess it is a bit embarrassing that it took several decades and a sick dog to drive that concept home. I pray that will be my mind-set for my remaining days. Live in the moment. Hannah demonstrates that simple and life-changing principle over and over.

Today she was sleeping soundly when I accidentally kicked a tennis ball near her bed. She raised up, saw the rolling ball, jumped up, and invited me to play. What a picture of spontaneity and joy! She was living completely and freely in the moment. She may have been achy and tired. But unexpectedly she had the chance to play with her friend. The message conveyed by her eyes and body language was clear: "Let's do this!"

At this point, I decided to experience fully the final journey Hannah and I had begun together and live fully in each moment. Let's go, my friend. Let's do this!

CHAPTER 5

UNLEASHED!

Nothing but love has made the dog lose his wild freedom,
to become the servant of man.

~ D. H. LAWRENCE

Journal Entry

Hannah loves the morning walk. When she sees me grab my walking shoes, she begins to vibrate with excitement. If the Department of Energy wants to find an untapped green energy source, it should harness Labrador tails. I think Hannah could power a small apartment building when she gets excited and that tail starts oscillating. I love the morning walk as well. It is a time to meditate, pray, listen to good music, and enjoy God's company.

The walk is pretty much the same each day for Hannah. She checks for new messages left by other canine friends along her social network. Sometimes she leaves a reply. She gets excited when she sees another

*person, dog, or anything breathing, really. Hannah
loves life.*

As I clipped the leash to Hannah's collar this morning, I couldn't help but notice her enthusiasm. She was happy just to get out and walk. The leash didn't spoil the anticipation of heading out the door, and despite its restriction, she still found abundant stimulation along the way.

When we got to the park, it was empty. As usual, we started out by a sign that sternly warned miscreants not to let their dogs run free. Today we were in temporary violation of city code 5544.

We entered a wooded area on the back side of the park where I felt comfortable letting Hannah run free. She became visibly energized by her liberation.

She ran ahead of me, spun around, and sprinted back. She spotted a squirrel several yards away and instinctively froze. Her body tensed in anticipation; she crouched down and took a few slow, deliberate steps, stalking her prey.

Then she bolted full throttle at the squirrel, ears flying in the wind.

The squirrel darted up a tree and Hannah stopped, looked up, and then turned with an expression of complete satisfaction as she trotted back toward me. She had a doggie smile from ear to ear. Hannah was fully alive when she was off the leash. Her freedom gave her such joy and energy. The squirrels weren't as keen with the idea.

When we reached the front part of the park, I called her and reattached the leash. Her body language was still happy, but there was not quite as much spring in her step. The leash again restricted her freedom.

Hannah's joyous foray into freedom made me think about

my journey with Jesus. I was introduced to faith in Christ in a church that put a legalistic leash on my daily Christian walk.

Our church leaders reminded me of characters from the movie *Monty Python and the Holy Grail.* We did not have the dreaded knights who said, "Ni." We had the dreaded pastors who said, "No."

I'm certain there were several volumes filled with things that were forbidden. Here is a sample platter of no-no's I was asked to follow.

NO movies.
NO drinking.
NO mixed swimming.
NO television.
NO cards.
NO rock-and-roll music.
NO smoking.
NO slacks for women.
NO long hair for men.
Corollary: NO short hair for women.

You get the idea. It's not surprising that it took me a long time to figure out grace and freedom in Christ. Ironically, there are a few noes in the New Testament that our moralists somehow overlooked. This little "no" verse would have come in handy (capitalization and italics added for emphasis).

There is *NO condemnation for those who belong to Christ Jesus.* And because you belong to him, the power of the life-giving Spirit has freed you from the power of sin that leads to death.

ROMANS 8:1-2

That would have been a refreshing mist of grace to our parched flock. Or how about these "no" verses (capitalization and italics added for emphasis)?

This is how love is made complete among us so that we will have confidence on the day of judgment: In this world we are like Jesus. There is *NO fear in love.* But perfect love drives out fear, because fear has to do with punishment. The one who fears is not made perfect in love. We love because he first loved us.

I JOHN 4:17-19, NIV

"Love the Lord your God with all your heart and with all your soul and with all your mind and with all your strength." The second is this: "Love your neighbor as yourself." There is *NO commandment greater than these.*

MARK 12:30-31, NIV

Love is patient and kind. Love is not jealous or boastful or proud or rude. It does not demand its own way. It is not irritable, and it keeps *NO record of being wronged.* It does not rejoice about injustice but rejoices whenever the truth wins out.

I CORINTHIANS 13:4-6

I have been crucified with Christ and I *NO longer live, but Christ lives in me.* The life I now live in the body, I live by faith in the Son of God, who loved me and gave himself for me. I do not set aside the grace of God, for if righteousness could be gained through the law, Christ died for nothing!

GALATIANS 2:20-21, NIV

That is a very different "no" list than the first one.

NO condemnation.
NO fear.
NO commandment greater than to love God and your
    neighbor.
NO record of wrongdoing when you love one another.
NO longer I who live but Christ who lives in me.

Hannah's foray off the leash reminded me again of my freedom from the burden of performance-based salvation. Remembering that restores the bounce in my step and spirit. In the freedom of grace, I am realizing and believing who God says I am. When I am unleashed by grace, I understand and trust who God says He is.

Like Hannah, I could live on my leash of moralism and get by fairly well. I did it for decades. Most of you wouldn't have noticed my constraints. I would still have fun and enjoy the journey, just as Hannah enjoyed the restricted part of her walk. But why should I accept partial freedom when God is offering complete freedom in His amazing grace?

Take off whatever leash is holding you back today and run freely in grace. Choose to believe that there is no condemnation in Christ for those who belong to Him. Don't settle for some self-imposed leash of performance. Hannah would tell you that the real blessing is running with complete freedom.

God's grace unhooks the leash and allows you to run unfettered and worship. God loves watching your exuberant liberation in Him. And He enjoys it when you turn and smile toward the heavens with complete satisfaction.

Enjoy the grace-filled romp of freedom just as Hannah

did. Walk (or run with ears flying) to Jesus. Approach Him with confidence, not in fear and shame. Having that relationship allows you to give up your burden of self-sufficiency and let Jesus lead. Thanks, Hannah, for helping me see that.

CHAPTER 6

GOOD FRIENDS

You really have to be some kind of a creep for a dog to reject you.

~JOE GARAGIOLA

Journal Entry

*Joni and I are going away for a few days. It will
be hard to leave Miss Hannah behind because we
just don't know when the cancer will rear its ugly
head. But it does give us a lot of comfort that we are
leaving her in the loving care of our son Scott and
his wife, Caroline. You might remember them as the
coconspirators who wonderfully brought Hannah into
our lives a decade ago. And it also gives us comfort
that Hannah will be hangin' with her best friend
Sadie. Nothing like good friends to ease separation
anxieties for all involved.*

Sadie. Just the mention of her best friend's name gets Hannah excited. From the moment we pull out of the driveway and head to Sadie's house (at least Sadie thinks it is hers), you can see Hannah's growing eagerness as we drive through the neighborhood. My canine navigator doesn't need a GPS for this familiar route. Her ears perk up and her tail begins to wag as we get closer.

When we arrive, she jumps out of the car and heads straight to the front door without the normal olfactory explorations. She bounces up and down because her sweet friend is on the other side. Suddenly, the door opens and the greeting is simple. There is no extensive sniffing or posturing; their body language is relaxed. They are two old girlfriends.

Watching how easily Hannah and Sadie settle in together is a hallmark of real friendship. Real friends come together as if time has never passed. Whether it's been hours, days, or years since you've been together, when you see a real friend, you immediately feel safety, comfort, and connection.

It was that way for me and my college buddy Rick when we finally got together—the first time in many years. We hugged, sat down, ordered some coffee, and reconnected as if we had hit the play button on a movie that had been paused for decades. We picked right up with the rhythm of our friendship. That is a friend.

Or when I hang out with my buddy Ed after weeks or months apart and we talk about everything and nothing. At the end of the day my self-worth bucket is filled and overflowing, yet when my lovely bride asks me what we talked about, I can't reconstruct thirty seconds of our conversation. That is a friend.

The advent of social media has accentuated the difference between friends and friendships. I have hundreds of

Facebook "friends," befriended with a click. It is easy to have friends who know what you like, listen to, and read. But it is hard work and risky to cultivate friendships with people who know who you are when the facade comes down.

Real friends are a treasure that we push way too far down the priority list. We sure think a lot about pursuing other treasures on our list. Too many of us don't prioritize the importance of building real friendships. Honestly, when you have a real crisis, would you rather have a promotion or a pal you could lean on? When heartaches come, would you prefer an award or an ally to walk with you?

In the grand scheme of life, you will have just a handful of real friends. Friends whom you can tell anything or say anything to and not be rejected. Friends who will drop everything when you need them.

Joni and I have many friends and that is a blessing. But the "real" friend roll call is pretty short. Relationships like that take time and investment. I believe you have to go through a variety of experiences together to really get to that next level of friendship. You don't really know a person until you go through adversity with him or her. That is not something you can plan or force. Cancer thinned our friend "herd" a bit as we learned who was there when we were at our worst. But God brought others into our lives who were willing to be real.

There is something powerfully healing and affirming about having someone in your life with whom you can drop the pretense. Many of us harbor the secret fear that if our friends found out everything that was true about us they would drop us in horrified indignation and run for the hills. But what if that is one more lie from the Deceiver? What if we could develop relationships of trust and grace where exactly the opposite occurred? What if the revelation of the truth about us caused our friends to love us more? What if we trusted a few with who we really are? I know some of you might be checking out right now because you have been deeply hurt by someone you trusted who did not deserve that trust. Hang with me. It is possible.

God designed this journey of life to be lived in community. It's the description of the early church.

> They joined with the other believers and devoted
> themselves to the apostles' teaching and fellowship,
> sharing in the Lord's Supper and in prayer. A deep
> sense of awe came over them all, and the apostles
> performed many miraculous signs and wonders. And
> all the believers met together constantly and shared
> everything they had. They sold their possessions and
> shared the proceeds with those in need. They worshiped
> together at the Temple each day, met in homes for the
> Lord's Supper, and shared their meals with great joy and
> generosity—all the while praising God and enjoying the
> goodwill of all the people. And each day the Lord added
> to their group those who were being saved.
>
> ACTS 2:42-47

We were created to be in a community with other believers. Because of our unity in Christ, we are to embrace those different from ourselves. That's what makes a church dynamic to a person who experiences grace and acceptance for the first time. And that is why church can be devastating when the congregation becomes selective, judgmental, and legalistic. Anne Lamott shares a thought-provoking observation: "You can safely assume you've created God in your own image when it turns out that God hates all the same people you do."[1]

That is both an ouch and an amen statement. When differences result in judgment, what we thought was a safe place instead becomes the biggest betrayal of all. When we become "experienced" Christians, something seems to happen. We can lose touch with our former brokenness and sinfulness and desperate need to be forgiven and accepted. That is when the pretense begins that our holiness is based on performance instead of complete dependence on Christ.

Years ago I wrote *When Bad Christians Happen to Good People.* I envisioned a church that would be the kind of place that you couldn't keep people away from even if you barred the doors. A place that would value every spiritual, physical, and financial gift, no matter how big or small. A place that would make it a practice to reach out and care for one another sacrificially. A place committed to meet those needs that we now prefer to leave to the "professional Christians" on staff. I dreamed of people from different walks of life, economic status, and culture being involved in each other's lives without our differences dividing us. A place that would practice the Prodigal Son ministry, running to welcome those returning home, especially those scarred by bad decisions and sin. We would hold our brothers and sisters accountable to godly standards, but always in humility and grace. We would delight in the company of other spiritual travelers and make it a priority that no one ever felt alone.

I realize now that what I was longing for was a place of grace.

I know that finding and living in real community in our culture isn't easy. I understand how easy it is to want to throw in the towel. I almost did. The truth is that we *need* community, even if we've been hurt by bad relationships in the past. If you aren't in a community of grace, it may be time to ask

God to lead you to such a place. I know that can be daunting. It took me a long time to find such a place, but I found one. It took me a longer time to realize how God was redeeming every hurt, every slight, and every trial. Eventually, I was able to see how He'd been preparing me, especially through those hard times, to embrace and welcome grace in a whole new way.

I have been swept away by grace. My life—including my relationship with Jesus, my marriage, and my ministry—has been transformed. It's been *that* dramatic.

So why aren't there more revelers on the grace train? And why are so many afraid to even board? I think part of the reason is that many of us don't want to give up what control we still feel we have. When you lean on grace, you surrender control, and that's not very appealing to many people, including Christians. When Christ asked us to love one another with all of our hearts, souls, and minds, He was asking us to give up our perceived rights to get even, keep score, and balance the scales. That feels scary and maybe even unfair to our American mind-set.

The apostle Peter showed us how that plays out on the ground.

> Above all, keep loving one another earnestly, since love covers a multitude of sins. Show hospitality to one another without grumbling. As each has received a gift, use it to serve one another, as good stewards of God's varied grace.
>
> I PETER 4:8-10, ESV

The need for church community is clear. But it's even more important to look at what Jesus modeled. Jesus knew hundreds of people. He traveled with dozens. He sent out seventy. He discipled twelve. And He invested deeply in three. Jesus' inner circle consisted of Peter, James, and John. He confided in these three men on a deeper and more profound level than any of the other disciples. I've found the same results in my own life. My greatest growth has taken place since I risked trusting a small group of men—three of them. The number wasn't by design; it just ended up being three.

Legendary professor Howard Hendricks of Dallas Theological Seminary said that every man needs three different types of individuals in his life: a Paul, a Barnabas, and a Timothy. Paul is the older man who will mentor you and offer you his experience. It has been hard for me to find older men these days, but I have been blessed with several over the years. Timothy is the young man whom you build into. But it's Barnabas whom I track with the most, aptly described by Hendricks.

> A Barnabas is a soul brother, somebody who loves you but is not impressed by you. Somebody to whom you can be accountable. Somebody who's willing to keep you honest, who's willing to say, "Hey, man, you're neglecting your wife, and don't give me any guff!"[2]

What a great description of a true friend. Someone who loves you but is not impressed by you. A person who takes the chance to tell you the truth, and you know it is because he or she wants only the best for you. That is how God desires our community to look. I can only receive real love from you to the extent that you know the truth about who I really am.

We all have blind spots in our hearts. I need a person who loves me enough to gently point them out.

I hope you will find the courage to carefully trust someone with everything that is true about you. Maybe it starts with you being that person for someone else, to begin to see how it looks in practice. Finding a friend can be daunting and even paralyzing. Being a friend is something that all of us can do.

There are a couple of things I have discovered about my deepest friends. First is that they understand the deep need for grace. When they understand how much they need the grace of Jesus, they are far more willing to give grace to others. The second characteristic is they love life. I need my most trusted friends to be fun loving. I have to enjoy spending time with a friend if I am going to open up my heart. I want to laugh and be silly, to balance out the hard work of relationship.

Clearly that was a dynamic in Hannah and Sadie's relationship. In the picture on page 44, I'm not sure what Hannah just shared with her friend, but Sadie got a big laugh out of it. Hannah actually looks like she might have said something a little inappropriate.

In 1937, Harvard University began a study to find the most important factors for human well-being and happiness. More than 250 male Harvard students who seemed healthy and well-adjusted were selected for a longitudinal study that would keep tabs on their lives for more than seventy years. The researchers factored in measurable items like physical exercise, cholesterol levels, marital status, the use of alcohol, smoking, education levels, and weight, but also more subjective psychological factors.

In 2009 someone asked Dr. George Vaillant, the director of the study, what he had learned about human happiness from the decades of data. The brilliant Harvard social scientist said what the apostle Paul had concluded a couple of millennia earlier: "The only thing that really matters in life are your relationships to other people."[3]

Paul added a layer or two to that equation by pointing out that no earthly possession or accomplishment is more important than the relationships in your life. Our culture tells us other things are just as important. Don't believe it. When I am on my deathbed, I am sure I will not ask to be dragged out to my new car so I can sit in the rich leather seats one last time. I am sure I will not want to look at the awards that I received a final time as I expire. I am sure I will not want to catch up on what is happening in social media with my several hundred "friends." I will want to be with those who matter the world to me.

Speaking of relationships, during our trip we checked in from time to time to see how Miss Hannah was faring. Scott reported that she seemed healthy and was definitely happy. No surprise there. She was hanging with her friend.

CHAPTER 7

RUN TO THE MASTER

You care for people and animals alike, O LORD.
How precious is your unfailing love, O God!

PSALM 36:6-7

As I write this, dog friend Hannah is nodding off while sitting upright. She is exhausted from following me everywhere I have gone during a thunderstorm that has been rumbling across the plains for several hours. If the thunder doesn't stop soon, she may pass out. I have petter's cramp from trying to comfort her during the storm. I like to think this is my chance to pay forward Hannah's unbridled adulation for me when I have accomplished great things like, well, coming in from getting the mail.

I have had some experience with big dogs and storms. Comparing crazy Charlie's manic response to Hannah's concerned dependence was instructive. During this storm, whenever I ambled to a stop, Hannah would plop next to me and lean most of her weight against me for reassurance and comfort.

She wanted to be wherever I was. It was not enough to be in the room with me. It was not enough to have visual contact. Hannah wanted to lean on me. She wanted to "feel" the presence of her master.

Her actions reminded me of a chorus from an old hymn we used to sing at church:

> *Leaning, leaning, safe and secure from all alarms. . . .*

I am not sure that Hannah felt secure, but I believe she did feel safer leaning into me, her provider and master. Her simple, instinctive desire was a good example of how I should react to life's storms. I looked up the lyrics for the rest of the hymn, which is based on Deuteronomy 33:27, "The eternal God is your refuge, and his everlasting arms are under you."

> *What a fellowship, what a joy divine,*
> *Leaning on the everlasting arms;*
> *What a blessedness, what a peace is mine,*
> *Leaning on the everlasting arms.*

> *Leaning, leaning, safe and secure from all alarms;*
> *Leaning, leaning, leaning on the everlasting arms.*

I think Hannah's simple act of trust in me provides a good foundation to prepare for any life storm. Run to the comfort of the Master.

We learn a lot about ourselves during the storms of life. Minister John Zahl sagely observed that "God's office is at the end of your rope."[1] I have found myself at the end of my personal rope and squarely in God's office on numerous occasions.

Storms are a necessary part of the refining program. Too often we view the storms as something to endure instead of a sovereignly directed opportunity to grow in grace and become more like Jesus. God loves us too much to give us only smooth sailing. That sounds crazy, but it is really logical when you think about how we mature. God gives us both good and bad things to help us mature spiritually. We have to lean into a sovereign God who sees exactly what we need to grow.

All followers of Christ wrestle with doubt when we are deep in the storm. Can we believe that trials are really tender mercies in disguise? That is exactly what David wrote in Psalm 119:71-77.

My suffering was good for me,
    for it taught me to pay attention to your decrees.
Your instructions are more valuable to me
    than millions in gold and silver.
You made me; you created me.
    Now give me the sense to follow your commands.
May all who fear you find in me a cause for joy,
    for I have put my hope in your word.
I know, O LORD, that your regulations are fair;
    you disciplined me because I needed it.
Now let your unfailing love comfort me,
    just as you promised me, your servant.
Surround me with your tender mercies so I may live,
    for your instructions are my delight.

Too many Christians have a theology more resembling karma than Christ. If I do this good thing, then good things should happen. If a bad thing happens, I must have done something bad in God's eyes. That is *not* the gospel.

Bad things happen to everyone. My desire is to automatically "lean in" to the One who can comfort me in my trials. Hannah does not try to figure out why the storm is happening. She does not doubt that I love her because she is in a frightening place. She wants to be completely with me until the storm passes by. What an example of how followers of Christ should respond in a storm. Lean on Jesus. Fully.

Joni loves pottery, so one of my "sacrificial" ways to love her is to accompany her to pottery shops. Guys refer to that as "hitting behind the runner" or "taking the charge." Once we visited a shop where the artisans were making vases and pots right before our eyes, surrounded by shelves of the colorful, beautiful, and functional finished products.

While Joni looked around, I watched a potter take a nondescript lump of clay and skillfully make a unique creation. This verse from Isaiah came to mind.

> O Lord, you are our Father.
> We are the clay, and you are the potter.
> We all are formed by your hand.
> ISAIAH 64:8

Okay, I'm starting to get it, Lord. I was fascinated by the complexity of the process. The potter must make sure that no dirt or impurities are in the clay. These unwanted materials will make the pot weak and unusable for its intended purpose. God desires to do the same with us.

Impurities (sin) weaken us and keep us from our intended purpose.

The potter kneads the clay to ensure that there are no air bubbles; otherwise the pot might crack when fired in the kiln. In my life, my "air bubbles" are pockets of resistance when I decide I must control my destiny instead of trusting God. I can appear to be molded and conformed to God's image, but I have unseen "bubbles" of pride and anger and control. These self-generated bubbles can cause me to crack under the heat of adversity.

The metaphors that Scripture uses are so powerful when we take the time to understand context and culture. The newly formed pottery, called "greenware," is carefully placed on a shelf to air-dry before the next step. It is brittle and easily broken. Something else needs to happen to permanently set the object's shape and make it strong and usable. The clay must endure the fire of the kiln.

Trials by fire can have that same effect on us as followers of Jesus. Trials can make us stronger and set our shape as His followers. Or, if we are unprepared, the fire of life's trials can cause us to crack and make us useless for His plan.

I can choose to be content in my "greenware" state, brittle and useless for service. But God knows that it is in the trials of fire that we are strengthened and most effective. It is nearly always in that uncomfortable adversity that the true beauty of our creative process is revealed. I cannot think of an instance of significant growth in my life that has happened without the refining heat of trials.

There are a couple of huge differences between the earthly potter and God as the Potter. When the earthly potter finds a bad piece of clay, he discards it. Our heavenly Potter patiently works with us even when we seem misshapen and worthless.

A shattered piece of pottery is often thrown out or repurposed in some way. Only our heavenly Father can take the shards of our brokenness and reshape us into something beautiful and effective for Him.

The words of the apostle James make more sense in the context of the Potter's process.

> Consider it pure joy, my brothers, whenever you face trials of many kinds, because you know that the testing of your faith develops perseverance.
>
> JAMES 1:2-3, NIV

There is no joy in the trial, but there is joy in the knowledge of how God uses such events in our lives. If you are in the midst of a trial or about to face a trial, take comfort that God desires for you to emerge strengthened and beautiful and useful. One potter said that the greatest thing about making pots is that each lump of clay has near-infinite potential. The lump of clay that is me and the lump of clay that is you have infinite potential because we have an infinite God who is patient and good. We should not fear or run from the dark moments. What happens when we walk through them is worth the cost.

Timothy Keller writes about this in his book *Walking with God through Pain and Suffering*.

> There is no way to know who you really are
> until you are tested. There is no way to really
> empathize and sympathize with other suffering
> people unless you have suffered yourself. There
> is no way to really learn how to trust in God
> until you are drowning.[2]

Because I suffered from loneliness as an adolescent, I learned how to empathize. When we went through the pain of losing our only daughter, Katie, to a birth defect, I was shown who I really was. Facing Joni's cancer showed me that only God can throw you a lifeline when you are drowning in a sea of fear and confusion. It was all of those things and more that teach me to lean into the strength of the Master during trials.

Hannah gave me a simple illustration today of what it looks like to lean on your master for comfort and strength. She had no other plan. I shouldn't either. Plans A, B, and C should be to first lean fully into the arms of my Master and loving Father. Of course, we have responsibilities during trials, but I am talking about the hard work of staying spiritually upright in a life storm. We need help beyond our own strength for that task.

It is not a natural reaction for us to lean on His everlasting arms when the storm comes. But if you do, you will find peace, joy, and safety.

What have I to dread, what have I to fear,
Leaning on the everlasting arms?
I have blessed peace with my Lord so near,
Leaning on the everlasting arms.

Hannah just passed out and is snoring. My work for now is finished, but the lessons are far from finished. Today Hannah reminded me to run to the Master when the storm hits and lean fully into God's comforting and everlasting arms. It is the only truly safe place to be. She runs to her master without doubt or question. Lord, teach me to do the same.

CHAPTER 8

SHAKE OFF THE LIES

Dogs never lie about love.

~JEFFREY MOUSSAIEFF MASSON

Journal Entry

*I can disappoint Hannah over and over. I can tell
her "no play," and minutes later she brings her toy
with hopeful anticipation in her eyes. I can ignore
her nuzzle and she lays down, takes a power nap, and
then optimistically tries again. How much healthier
would our relationships be if we could make our
needs known but not get angry and isolate ourselves
if they are not met? If I am rejected, I tend to keep
score. When the score reaches my preset "game over"
point, I get angry or go off to pout. Note to self: let
your needs be known with grace and love and without
keeping score.*

Hannah never keeps score. I might ignore her invitation to play fifteen times in a row, and she will not change her approach one bit. I might brush away her attempts to nuzzle all morning long, and she will be back after lunch with hopeful eyes and wagging tail.

It is not a sin to have and express needs that others can meet. It is also not a sin when another person cannot meet my needs right when I ask. Paul made the convicting observation that love does not keep score in his famous love passage to the church at Corinth.

It does not demand its own way. It is not irritable,
and it keeps no record of being wronged.

I CORINTHIANS 13:5

Paul just dismissed my only viable math skill.

Today a routine pastime for Hannah led to a not-so-routine response from her human student. Many times I am grateful there are no video cameras archiving our daily activities. Sometimes the stupid things I do are accidental, but too often they are premeditated.

This morning's foray to the pool with Hannah generated one of those self-inflicted embarrassing moments. Hannah loves to retrieve tennis balls from the pool, and she prefers to bring each one out of the water, proudly present it to me, and then dash back in again. Each time she comes out of the water she shakes, releasing an impressive torrent of spray.

I wonder how she does that. Comedian Mike Birbiglia has a line that he uses when the audience anticipates his next not-so-brilliant move. "I know," he deadpans, "some of you are in the future too." Yep. I tried to see if

I could shake water off me. I started with a modest goal. *Can I shake some of the water off the graying mane?* I submerged my noggin, came up, and shook my head vigorously. Hannah looked on, puzzled. Hardly a drop of water moved. I did accomplish getting a crick in my neck and a mild headache.

The answer to my epically failed attempts was pretty simple. I lacked the power to shake off the water, unlike Hannah, who, like every other dog, had a God-given ability to shake it off. Later I pondered my sanity and Hannah's talent.[1]

As much as I enjoyed my little experiment, the life lesson from Hannah was not how to shake off water. What I need to learn is how she can shake off rejection and disappointment *way* better than I can. If I say no, Hannah doesn't get insecure and touchy. When she is rejected, she doesn't start wondering why she is not good enough. She doesn't hear condemning barks from her puppyhood. She doesn't flash back to her littermates mocking her with cruel yips. She doesn't think, *Maybe Dad doesn't like that toy; if I bring his favorite toy I'm sure he won't be able to resist.* Hannah doesn't slink away and hide, thinking she is worthless if I don't respond. She simply accepts that now is not the time and communicates through her body language and gaze that everything's okay—she's cool with me. *Oh, and by the way, I'll be back soon.* Hannah doesn't shut down. She simply tries again, with self-image undaunted.

Not so for me. I immediately hear the voices of condemnation when I am rejected or someone is angry at me. I couldn't think of any verses about shaking off water, but I did recall a verse from Hebrews about "shaking" or "throwing" off those things that cause us to stumble.

> Since we are surrounded by such a great cloud of
> witnesses, let us throw off everything that hinders and
> the sin that so easily entangles.
>
> HEBREWS 12:1, NIV

When she climbs out of the pool, Hannah has definitely learned how to throw off the water that hinders her. I love the imagery of getting up and shaking off all the things (even some good things) that hinder me from an intimate relationship with God.

Did you catch the part that it is *not only sin* that entangles us? That is what I tended to dwell on—to "get better" for God and be more "righteous." But the verse says to throw off *any* weight or encumbrance. In order for me to be used most effectively for God, that good thing that is not the best thing has to go. As Timothy Keller explains perfectly, "An idol is a good thing turned into an ultimate thing."[2]

Here is the rest of the Hebrews passage read with that eye-opening definition of idolatry in mind.

> Let us run with perseverance the race marked out for
> us. Let us fix our eyes on Jesus, the author and perfecter
> of our faith, who for the joy set before him endured
> the cross, scorning its shame, and sat down at the right
> hand of the throne of God. Consider him who endured
> such opposition from sinful men, so that you will not
> grow weary and lose heart.
>
> HEBREWS 12:1-3, NIV

I am drawn to wounded and dysfunctional people like a moth to light. When I hear their stories, I see a familiar pattern. They tend to believe that all the old junk in their lives is still true about them in God's eyes. Too many followers of Jesus cannot believe they are a new and holy creation. Recently I saw a T-shirt with this message: EVEN IF THE VOICES IN MY HEAD AREN'T REAL THEY DO HAVE SOME GOOD IDEAS. I got an initial chuckle out of that one. But then I thought, *Wait! The voices in* my *head rarely have good ideas.*

I suspect that is true for some of you as well. Sadly, the voices in our heads are real, formidable foes, voices that were programmed from childhood. Negative comments from parents, teachers, coaches, siblings, friends, fellow Christians, and assorted others have laid down deeply grooved tracks in my self-image sound track mix. Favorite cuts like these are always cued and ready to be played.

"You will never change."
"What were you thinking?"
"I can't believe you did that again."
"What is wrong with you?"
"I am so disappointed in you."

And the number one accusation on my personal Top 10 countdown . . .

"How could you be so stupid?"

That one cued up and replayed just this weekend when I locked my rental car keys in the trunk. When you mess up, the voices begin. And then your own voice joins the chorus. "It is true. I am not worthy. I am not enough. I am stupid. I don't deserve to be loved."

When you face disappointment, rejection, failure, loss, and trials, self-incriminating remarks flood your mind.

> "Why wasn't I a better (pick one) spouse/friend/brother/
> sister/relative?"
> "If I had done (insert action), this would not have
> happened."
> "Why didn't I (insert missed opportunity) when I had
> the chance?"
> "Why did I (pick one or more) work too much/travel
> too much/whatever too much when I should have
> been there?"

If I may lean on my sports background here, Satan calls the all-out blitz when people of faith go through seasons of trial and doubt. He delights in accusing and trying to rock the very foundation of your faith. Satan is, always has been, and always will be a liar. You have learned to never trust a liar at work or in other relationships. How much more should we pray to recognize and reject the lies that Satan attacks us with during adversity?

There is another voice. It is much softer and requires more effort to hear. It is not a voice of shame. It is a voice of hope, love, acceptance, forgiveness, and grace. You have to slow way down and be quiet to hear this voice.

Jesus had to deal with Satan's lies face-to-face. Three times He was tempted by the devil's alluring promises (see Matthew 4:1-11). The very men whom Jesus invested His heart, soul, and life into heard that lying voice too, and made ungodly suggestions. James and John wanted to call down fire from heaven to destroy a town that did not welcome them. Jesus rebuked them.

Peter got his hair parted when he tried to explain to Jesus that the events the Lord had just outlined (His imminent suffering and death) really couldn't happen.

Peter took him aside and began to reprimand him for saying such things. "Heaven forbid, Lord," he said. "This will never happen to you!" Jesus turned to Peter and said, "Get away from me, Satan! You are a dangerous trap to me. You are seeing things merely from a human point of view, not from God's." Then Jesus said to his disciples, "If any of you wants to be my follower, you must turn from your selfish ways, take up your cross, and follow me."

MATTHEW 16:22-24

All of us hear those voices from the enemy. The voices from bad experiences in our past may require counseling to help erase them. But for the everyday challenges of the journey, I have learned that the voice we tend to hear first in the spiritual battle is the loud one. Step back, be still, and listen for the quiet voice of the Holy Spirit.

Of course you could have done more in that relationship. That's the benefit of hindsight. Of course you could have responded better at times. Who is not guilty of those accusations? Yet God's love is unfailing. Our God is a God of forgiveness. We need to fix our eyes on Jesus. Don't lose heart. Don't allow the enemy to keep you from leaning on God for comfort because of your shame. That is not from the Lord.

Those voices of past sin and failures and hurt are no longer who you are. The voices of accusation that you might hear when facing loss and trials don't define you anymore. You need to "shake off" those voices like Hannah shakes off the post-swim water, then take it a step further.

Hannah loves her post-swim towel ritual. The moment she sees me pick up the towels, she comes running. I wrap her up in their softness and give her a brisk rubdown to finish the drying job.

We need help as well. We need to wrap ourselves not in towels but in robes of righteousness placed on us by our Lord. And we need the help of our Christian friends to affirm that truth.

When I deny Hannah her desire for affection or play, she shakes it off and comes back later, believing that I will respond. There are no voices of shame in her canine brain. She lives in the moment, expecting the best from her master. When I do not deliver, she accepts me with uncommon grace. I would do well to follow her lead.

CHAPTER 9

TRUST . . . THE CURRENCY OF LOVE

Dogs have given us their absolute all. We are the center of their universe.
We are the focus of their love and faith and trust. They serve us in return
for scraps. It is without a doubt the best deal man has ever made.

~ROGER CARAS

Journal Entry

My canine friend Hannah is completely willing to surrender to me, her master. She trusts me completely. Today started early. Really early. Really, really early. I was blessed with the chance to watch grandson Ethan for the day, and my precious boy lives about two hours away. Hannah was going to take the road trip with me to his house. I woke up at 4:30 a.m. and Hannah did not stir.

I hit the shower and dressed without any movement from her. She was used to this routine from countless trips I had taken before. I wake early, get ready, and leave. None of this routine normally involved her, so Hannah wisely chose to sleep.

As I headed out the door, I softly called her. She raised her head and looked a bit confused. Me? This is not how this normally works. Again I gently called her. She got up, stretched, and followed me out the door.

When we got to the car Hannah looked at me momentarily. *Are you sure about this? Should I really be here?* I coaxed her to jump in the car, and she quickly did. Soon we settled in for the two-hour drive, Hannah nestled beside me, placing her full trust in my actions.

When I asked her to follow me, she had no idea where I was going or what was in store for her. She knew this was unusual, but that didn't deter her. I didn't have to beg, cajole, or pull her into the front seat. I didn't have to give any explanations or bribe her with a treat or toy. She trusted me, following me out of the room, out of the house, into the darkness, and toward the unknown.

That is the kind of trust that we can have in someone who is trustworthy. Jesus asks us to trust Him with the same unquestioning attitude children possess. He isn't asking us to be childish or immature. He is asking us to follow Him with childlike faith.

One day some parents brought their children to Jesus so he could touch and bless them. But the disciples scolded the parents for bothering him. When Jesus saw what was happening, he was angry with his disciples. He said to them, "Let the children come to me. Don't stop them! For the Kingdom of God belongs to those who are like these children. I tell you the truth, anyone who

doesn't receive the Kingdom of God like a child will never enter it." Then he took the children in his arms and placed his hands on their heads and blessed them.
MARK 10:13-16

When Hannah and I arrived at Ethan's house, I scooped up my grandson and held him over my head. He giggled in excitement. He never once worried that he was about nine feet above a brick floor. He trusted me. He never asked for my babysitter credentials or proof that I had never dropped any children in my life. He trusted me. When his mom, Holly, left for her appointments, she didn't panic that Ethan would be left without protection or nourishment. She trusted me.

There were two aspects of trust at work here. My grandson trusted me instinctively as a child. His mom trusted me as a dad who had raised three boys including her own beloved husband, Matt. The same proves true with God. We are to trust our heavenly Father instinctively as the One who loves us, and we can trust Him because we have the testimony of others about His love and care.

Hannah lives in complete trust of me. If only it were as easy for me to do the same with my Master. Surrendering my will to a much kinder and more knowledgeable Master than Hannah relates to can be a battle for me. I get caught up in self-protection, fear, and shame. I have the advantage of opposable thumbs to read the Bible, so I know from His Word that God is trustworthy. And yet I still have a hard time when God asks me to follow Him into the unknown.

When I have trust issues, I decide to go my own way. I was pondering that fine trait of mine the following morning as I walked with Hannah. I imagined how Jesus might look at my recent doubts and subsequent AWOL tendencies. It was time to imagine a one-on-one conversation with Jesus, set in the local caffeine café.

WWJO? (What Would Jesus Order?) Based on what I have gleaned from the ancient texts, I pipe up, "One grande extra-shot Americano, please, for my Friend and I'll take the same with room." We found our way to the table and then He spoke. . . .

> **Jesus:** *I've missed spending time with you recently.*
> **Dave:** *I've been really busy with work and traveling.*
> **Jesus:** *I'm available 24-7.*
> **Dave:** *Yeah. I know.*
> **Jesus:** *I was glad you came to Me with that fear you were dealing with last week.*
> **Dave:** *I don't know how I could have handled that without You.*
> **Jesus:** *I'm here for you. But you know I'm also here when there is not a crisis going on in your life.*
> **Dave:** *I know. I forget that sometimes. I get so busy that I don't have time to spend with You.*
> *[Jesus takes a sip of the grande extra-shot Americano, and from the look on His face is obviously enjoying it.* Whew! Got that one right!*]*
> **Jesus:** *I was just wondering something.*
> **Dave:** *What?*
> **Jesus:** *[He smiles warmly.] Did you find time to spend on your fantasy football team roster over the past few days?*
> **Dave:** *Do You need another Americano? Pastry?*
> **Jesus:** *Nice try. You make time for what is important to you. You know I am not condemning you. I just want to be as important to you as you are to Me. I miss you.*

Dave: *Why do You put up with me?*
Jesus: *Because I love you. I always have. And I always will. Even when you are worrying about your fantasy football starters instead of finding time for Me. By the way, you should have started the running back.*

I don't know about you, but I wonder if an actual face-to-face conversation with Jesus would change how I go about my daily routines. I suspect that such a little talk would energize my walk with Him. So the next question is simple and convicting. Why isn't that already happening on a consistent basis? I have His words and teachings to study. I have the presence of the Holy Spirit in my life. I have other followers of Jesus to share the journey with each day. I have everything I need to become one of Jesus' success stories. So why don't I do it?

I think I falter because I make faith and trust entirely too complicated. Jesus didn't say figure out every theological jot and tittle. (Note to spiritual hall monitors: there is an important place for that discipline. No e-mails, please.) Jesus didn't say, "Go and clean up your act, and I will deem you a worthy follower." He didn't say, "Browbeat yourself and others into behaving better in order to earn the badge of righteousness." He simply said,

"Follow me."

Not once. Pretty regularly.

"Come, follow me," Jesus said, "and I will make you fishers of men."
MATTHEW 4:19, NIV

Jesus told him, "Follow me."
MATTHEW 8:22

[Jesus said,] "If anyone would come after me, he must deny himself and take up his cross and follow me."
MATTHEW 16:24, NIV

[Jesus answered,] "Come, follow me."
MATTHEW 19:21

Finding Philip, he said to him, "Follow me."
JOHN 1:43, NIV

[Jesus replied,] "Whoever serves me must follow me."
JOHN 12:26, NIV

Jesus answered, "If I want him to remain alive until I return, what is that to you? You must follow me."
JOHN 21:22, NIV

"Follow me," he told him, and Matthew got up and followed him.
MATTHEW 9:9, NIV

Thank you, Matthew, for being like Hannah—no hesitation, just trust.

In the immortal words of Forrest Gump, "I'm not a smart man." But like Forrest I have a keen sense of the obvious. Jesus is saying to follow Him. That takes childlike trust on my part. The rest of it we will figure out together as I follow Him in complete trust.

I am, even if you are kind in your evaluations, a slow

learner. I cannot believe how long it took me to even begin to understand God's grace and how much freedom that gives me. But to begin to live out of that truth, I had to trust it. I have a living, breathing, fur-covered example of trust living in my own home. Hannah has been a patient guide dog leading me through my trust blindness.

At the end of our visit in Waco, I loaded up the car. "C'mon, girl." Hannah didn't hesitate. Without the slightest indecision, she hopped in the car and snuggled into her blanket.

I should have no fear when Jesus asks me to follow Him. When He says, "Follow Me," the response should be simple. "Let's go."

CHAPTER 10

LIVE OUT OF WHO YOU ARE

*In order to really enjoy a dog, one doesn't merely try to
train him to be semihuman. The point of it is to open
oneself to the possibility of becoming partly a dog.*

~EDWARD HOAGLAND

Journal Entry

Today was day number 212 since we opted for Hannah's operation. The morning was crisp, sunny, and inviting for the daily walk. My canine friend is not yet showing overt symptoms of the cancer. Perhaps she sleeps a bit more during the day, but just putting on the walking shoes and warm clothes causes Hannah to vibrate. She runs from the bathroom to the living room and back to show her impatience with my pace of preparation. Running to the door, she stands and eagerly awaits the daily walk. She may not be fully healthy, but she is fully alive.

Even though Hannah knows the drill after nine years, she never approaches her daily walk in a ho-hum manner or seems bored with its predictability. Immediately her nose goes to the ground as she strides and devours the scents along the way. As I watch her I wonder, *What would it be like to have her sense of smell? On the one hand, it would be wonderful; on the other hand, not so much.* I'm brought to a sudden stop. Hannah has found an interesting odor that she must dig in and focus intently upon to decode.

Hannah is fully alive today. Each of us always has the ability to be fully alive, even when things are not going well for us physically. Andrew Peterson wrote a powerful song, "Queen of Iowa," about a dying woman who "with all of the things she was dying of, she was more alive than the others."[1]

I gently nudged Hannah on her way and she caught up to my pace. We passed a couple of neighborhood dogs who ran along the fence and barked furiously at us. Hannah's expression seemed bemused at their waste of energy. She is neither a barker nor a chaser—she is a retriever. That is her DNA. When a ball is thrown she chases the ball, brings it back, drops the ball, and waits to repeat her calling. Her instincts tell her to gently hold the object she retrieves in her mouth. She has been genetically programmed to know that biting hard on the object could damage it.

She was predestined to swim, run, and retrieve. That is the destiny of any retriever. Hannah does not try to be anything else. Even as a puppy, she chased anything we tossed her way and eagerly brought it back. We did not have to spend one minute training her. It was as natural as breathing for Hannah. Retrieving was her purpose and passion.

That was the lesson for today from my four-legged mentor.

I have also been created with a purpose. In fact, every person has a God-designed destiny whether they believe it or not. Henri Nouwen wrote about living with that frame of mind.

> We seldom realize fully that we are sent to fulfill God-given tasks. . . . We act as if we were simply dropped down in creation and have to decide how to entertain ourselves until we die. But we were sent into the world by God, just as Jesus was. Once we start living our lives with that conviction, we will soon know what we were sent to do.[2]

Living out of who you are is liberating. The apostle Paul had some thoughts about such a life when he wrote to the church at Ephesus.

> God saved you by his grace when you believed. And you can't take credit for this; it is a gift from God. Salvation is not a reward for the good things we have done, so none of us can boast about it. *For we are God's masterpiece. He has created us anew in Christ Jesus, so we can do the good things he planned for us long ago.*
> EPHESIANS 2:8-10, EMPHASIS ADDED

Think about that! You were rescued from the death of sin by grace. It was a gift that could not be earned. And you are a new creation, indeed a *masterpiece* for whom *good things* were planned *long ago*. How can followers of Jesus possibly have self-image issues? When we believe the lies.

I was created to be in fellowship with God and glorify Him. I have a God-given destiny. When I became a follower of Christ, my spiritual DNA was fundamentally changed.

I was forgiven. I became a new creation. I was given the righteousness of Jesus and the comfort and direction of the Holy Spirit. But I do not always live out of who I am. As my friends at Truefaced[3] say so beautifully, God doesn't want me to change. I have already been changed. He wants me to live out of *what is now true about me.* Hannah is helping me to understand the folly of trying to live out of a false identity.

Living authentically means I am honest with God and others about my sin. But my pride tries to "spin" what I want others to believe about me. I cover up my sin, acting like everything is okay. I give the illusion that I am in control. My need to manage my image is wrong and counterproductive to living for Jesus. I know that I should trust, but too often I try to "help" God with some astute advice on how He might accomplish His purpose for me. That is as foolish as Hannah sitting by and expecting me to chase the ball. Or me dropping her off in a field full of cattle and waiting impatiently for her to herd them into the corral. That is not who she is. I can sit there—wait for it—until the cows come home, and she will not be a herder.

When I first began to write down these thoughts about facing loss and lessons from my canine friend, I heard one of those voices that I mentioned in chapter 8. "You know, you could probably appeal to more readers if you lightened up on the Jesus stuff." I listened. *Hmmm. Maybe I should go a bit easier on the Jesus angle. Polls show that over 90 percent of people believe in God in some form, but not everyone is crazy about Jesus. Maybe the voice is right. What if I made these musings a bit more universal? Maybe I could sell more books and have some financial security.*

Today's lesson brought me to my senses. Processing life and loss through my faith in Christ is who I am. I should and I must live out of that truth, without compromising who I am.

It is completely effortless for Hannah to live out of who she is. For me, it's not as easy; I consistently fight for control. I feel the need to try to figure out God's will instead of just living in dependence on Him and letting His Spirit direct my paths. I try to show God how much I bring to the table, and I attempt to please Him by doing more. That makes as much sense as Hannah thinking she can drive the car.

(How ridiculous. She can't reach the accelerator and she has no insurance.)

Oh, sorry. I meant it is ridiculous to think that I can please God by strenuous efforts to prove my righteous zeal. I please God by trusting Him more. I can't earn it by my performance.

Hannah finds joy every day in simply living out of what she was created to be. Chasing a ball and bringing it back. Enjoying the exhilaration of a walk and the scents along the way. Nuzzling her human friends for a scratch or back rub.

I want to learn such effortless living, content to be who I was created to be. I want to find exhilaration in simply walking with God. To be joyous living in community with His wounded flock, helping as we limp forward together and loving them back to health. I want to stop regularly to enjoy the scents, sights, and majesty of nature. I desire to be tenderhearted and take every opportunity to hug and love those God has blessed me to be in relationship with on this planet.

In his book *The Cure*, written with Bruce McNicol and Bill Thrall, John Lynch sums up one of our greatest fears. "No one told me that when I wear a mask, only my mask receives love."[4] Haven't you feared that? *If I take off the mask, they will not like me, let alone love me.* In fact, genuine relationship only happens when you take off the mask and allow others to love you.

When you reveal your true self, your loved ones see the real you and not some phony performer trying to work through struggles by acting the way mature believers are "supposed" to respond. Without your mask, they see how you are really doing. *Only then* can others know how to love you well. You don't have to be "brave" or "fine" or "stalwart." You are allowed to be sad or lonely or depressed. That is part of the human condition.

Faith does not dehumanize us. We still feel, hurt, cry, get down, go through lengthy dry spells, and have bad hair days. When you are vulnerable about how you are really feeling, others can know how to pray, love, and walk with you through the valley. It gives them a chance to enter into honest community with you. C. S. Lewis noted that friendship begins at that moment when one person says to another, "What! You too? I thought I was the only one."[5] When your mask is removed, you visibly connect with others. They see your honest need and can relate to that need in love.

Take off the mask. Drop the pretense and accept who you are and where God has placed you. Live out of who you are. Hannah models it for me every day. She does not wake up determined to be a herder through sheer grit and discipline. She lives out of who she was created to be.

I am tired of waking up determined through grit and discipline to be righteous. Jesus says I already am. I am redeemed. A saint. So I am learning to believe who Jesus says I am and live out of that truth. The good news? It is freedom. And when you live effortlessly out of what is true about you, it's easy to find rest. Right, girl?

CHAPTER 11

GRATITUDE STARTS WITH ATTITUDE

If you pick up a starving dog and make him prosperous, he will not bite you. This is the principal difference between a dog and a man.

~MARK TWAIN, IN *PUDD'NHEAD WILSON*

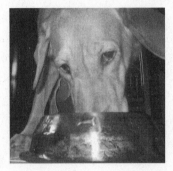

Every morning the routine is the same. Hannah pulls herself reluctantly from her comfy dog bed, stretches, and haltingly heads to the door. We share that extreme reluctance to start the day. She slowly heads outside to take care of business. We don't share that part of the routine. Often she will stop, turn, and look back toward the door. Once the morning business is completed, she transforms. She turns, picks up the pace from a saunter, to a quick walk, to an all-out dash to get back in the house. It is breakfast time!

Breakfast is an exciting event for Miss Hannah. Her eyes light up with anticipation. She watches my every move and inches forward impatiently if I get distracted. After all, in her mind, it is my most important task of the day. Or at least until dinnertime. When the food hits the dish, she tenses up and looks at me. I give the signal, and she dives in like the pie-eating champ at the county fair.

After feeding Hannah today, I took a moment to consider the source of her giddy anticipation. When we first heard about Hannah's diagnosis, I did some research and found that canine cancer sometimes progresses more slowly by eliminating carbs. So we switched exclusively to a high-protein, high-fat diet. That is what she has consumed every single day since.

This was day 274, so she was now staring at the same food in her dish for the 547th time. Yet Hannah still bounces up and down with excitement, her tail thumping nearby objects as I measure out the kibble. If I pause long enough, she actually begins to drool.

Whenever I place her dish in front of her, Hannah waits, giving me a certain look. *Does she want me to say grace?* I can't read her dog body language. No matter. She does seem grateful to have her dish refilled with the same old meal.

I don't mind leftovers, but I am pretty sure that somewhere around the fifth or sixth consecutive time you placed lasagna in front of me, I would start grumbling. Forget about the 500th time.

As Hannah happily devoured her morning manna, I realized she was demonstrating another life lesson—the importance of daily gratitude. Lack of gratitude is not a modern problem. Seventeenth century Anglican priest and English poet, George Herbert, summed it up when he penned this plea: "Thou that hast giv'n so much to me, / Give one thing more, a grateful heart."[1] Hannah demonstrates it every morning, day and night. Me? Not so much.

I readily accept blessings: "Thank you, Lord!" But when things go wrong, what is the first thing that pops into my mind? *Why me, Lord?*

I suspect that most of us have cried out to God with that same question, followed up by something along the lines of "I don't deserve for this to happen to me. Look at everything I do for You, God!"

During my morning walk with Miss Hannah, a song by Kris Kristofferson ran through my mind. "Why Me" has been one of my favorites, ever since my days as a young believer back in 1973. (If you do the math, you realize that I am not such a young believer anymore.) Kristofferson wrote the song during a low time in his personal life. He doesn't ask God why He allows bad things to happen, but rather questions why he has been given so many undeserved blessings. "What have I ever done to deserve even one of the pleasures I've known?"

So true. What have I done to deserve even one of God's blessings? I did not deserve forgiveness. That was a gift of grace from a loving God. I did not deserve to be born in the United States into incredible comfort, religious freedom, and opportunity. I did not deserve to be born healthy and moderately intelligent when others live with chronic pain and illness. All these things were blessings that I received without complaining to my Creator. The "Why me, Lord?" question we so often ask should have an entirely different focus.

"Why me, Lord? What have I done to deserve Your blessing?"

The answer is humbling. Nothing. It is true that some people seem to suffer a disproportionate amount of affliction and difficulty, which doesn't seem fair to our Western mindset. The theology that faithful Christians will experience nonstop prosperity, perfect health, and green lights at every intersection is a lie from the pit of hell. Job had a pretty good excuse to be angry and blame God. His wife even advised him to throw in the spiritual towel.

> His wife said to him, "Are you still trying to maintain your integrity? Curse God and die."
> But Job replied, "You talk like a foolish woman. Should we accept only good things from the hand of God and never anything bad?" So in all this, Job said nothing wrong.
>
> JOB 2:9-10

. . .

Tom Cuppett, my basketball coach at Chillicothe High School in southern Ohio, was a winner—a great teacher and motivator. He was instrumental in shaping me as a man. But Coach yelled at me a lot. It seemed I could never do anything right. We would run a play and the whistle would blow. "Burchett . . . what are you doing?" He would grab me and the other forwards and walk us through what was supposed to happen.

After my senior season Coach Cuppett called me into his office. "I have to let you in on something. Remember how I always yelled at you and walked you through the plays?"

I smiled. "Pretty hard to forget that you can't do anything right."

"The truth is that most of the time it was Jimmy (not his real name) who messed up and not you," Coach Cuppett confided. "He couldn't take the criticism and you could. So I yelled at you and then grabbed him and walked both of you through the plays so he would learn without losing his confidence."

"It would have been nice to know why I was the target so often."

"I couldn't tell you at the time. But I trusted you to keep going. And you did. Your ability to handle adversity made him and our team better."

During those high school years I accepted what I had to endure to achieve our goal of winning, even though I wasn't keen on Coach Cuppett's methods at the time. I was proud when I found out that I had gained honor in his eyes by trusting him even when things didn't seem "fair." How much more can I trust a God who loved me enough to offer grace when I was completely without merit? What if that trial is given to me because God knows I will remain steadfast and faithful and that He will be honored? What if I get called into God's office someday and find out that He gave me the gift of trials to reflect His glory, and now my rewards will far exceed that temporary pain? If I can trust an earthly coach, then I can certainly trust my heavenly Father with all of me.

My friend Ed Underwood says it well in his book *When God Breaks Your Heart.*

> Could it be that part of the answer to your question *"Why not me?"* is that Jesus is doing something more wonderful than you ever imagined? Is it possible that your heartache is designed to bring glory to the Savior in a way so unique and breathtaking that this is the only way? That's [the apostle] John's point: Jesus never messes with His followers.[2]

I love that. *Jesus never messes with His followers.* It is easy to grow complacent about gratitude for the little blessings of everyday life. It really gets tough to be grateful when life sucker punches you. For me, I think this line from C. S. Lewis sums up how such a response can be possible.

> We ought to give thanks for all fortune: if it is "good," because it is good, if "bad" because it works in us patience, humility and contempt of this world and the hope of our eternal country.[3]

The hope of our eternal country. What a beautiful thought for a follower of Jesus.

This is not our home. Joni and I could have chosen bitterness when our only daughter, Katie, was born with a terminal birth defect. Or we could choose gratitude that she lived for many months longer than expected and blessed us in ways we could not have imagined during that agonizing early tsunami of grief. We could be angry that her birth defect was not something that could be fixed by modern medicine. Or we could be grateful that she was completely healed when she went to that eternal country. God redeemed Katie's life in amazing ways that we could not have seen in our initial blinding grief.

We had a choice to make when our daughter was born with a neural tube defect and only lived fourteen months. We dealt with doubts, anger, and grief. We were profoundly sad. But we chose to trust God in the storm. We claim no great spiritual strength or maturity. We were scared and relying on the only source of strength that we could find.

One person responds to tragedy with deeper faith. Another turns from God in anger, perhaps never to return. What is the difference? Perhaps this parable that Jesus related in Matthew's Gospel offers the biggest clue. When the storm hits, what matters most is the foundation that you have built your faith upon.

Anyone who listens to my teaching and follows it is wise, like a person who builds a house on solid rock. Though the rain comes in torrents and the floodwaters rise and the winds beat against that house, it won't collapse because it is built on bedrock. But anyone who hears my teaching and doesn't obey it is foolish, like a person who builds a house on sand. When the rains and floods come and the winds beat against that house, it will collapse with a mighty crash.

MATTHEW 7:24-27

I have dealt with loss by relying on both types of foundations. My early theology was built on the shifting sand of self-effort and discipline. When the storm came, my "house of faith" collapsed like a house of cards. When I began to build on a foundation of identity and trusting who God is, my house of faith weathered the storm without being completely destroyed. The storm battered me full force, but the house stood.

What is that foundation made of? I would suggest that these are the foundation stones.

God is all powerful.
God is all knowing.
God is love.
God is holy.
God is good.
God is just.
God is righteous.
God is grace.
God is sovereign.
God is unchanging.

God is joy.

God is forgiving.

God is truth.

God is patient.

Start building from the foundation of who God says He is in Scripture. In 2008 Steven Curtis Chapman and his wife, Mary Beth, lost their daughter, Maria, in a heartbreaking accident. The singer/songwriter went back to the biblical foundation and reflected on the attributes of God as he wrestled with where God was when the tragedy happened. The result a year later, *Beauty Will Rise*, includes a cut called "God Is It True (Trust Me)"; Chapman concludes that if all that the Bible says is true, then God is whispering to trust Him, no matter what happens.

Our Western culture demands answers. We feel the need and even the right to understand why something happens. Is God totally sovereign, or do I have complete free will? Logic says one or the other must be true. God says both are true. We can't fathom that so we pick a side.

The same thing happens with tragedy. We can't understand how a loving God can allow heartbreaking tragedy. We question His goodness. But imagine that God was there with Maria Chapman when she was killed. Imagine that He wrapped His arms around her and called her by name as He lovingly escorted her to paradise with Him. We cannot understand how God can take the cruelty of this fallen planet and redeem it for good. But He can. We saw it with our daughter, Katie, whose story has touched thousands. Steven and Mary Beth Chapman have helped hundreds of thousands navigate the crushing blow of losing a child. The eternal impact of little Maria Chapman is incalculable. God redeemed that sadness. Maria awaits her parents and siblings in Glory. But there was still crushing sadness. The Chapmans chose to trust God in their anguish.

If the gospel message is true—and I believe it is—then God says to trust Him. His ways are not our ways, and His timing is certainly not ours, but His love is real. If you need proof, consider the Cross where God watched His Son scream out in agony even when He had the power to stop it.

Remember what Christ did at the Cross. Because of Jesus you have been given all these gifts of grace.

Forgiveness of past, present, and future sins
A brand-new identity
Righteousness
The Holy Spirit
A clean slate
Eternal life with God in heaven

All these gifts of grace are done deals that are completely ours without any fine print or catch. Coupling the attributes of God with the grace gifts of the gospel creates a foundation that can weather some category 5 life hurricanes. Believing who God says He is, understanding that I have been changed because of Christ, and living out of those two fundamentals are changing how I deal with adversity and loss.

It all starts with simple gratitude. This morning after breakfast I experienced another illustration of the principle. The weather was miserable. Cold, damp, bone-chilling winds made the idea of a morning walk less than attractive. Yet I looked into the expectant eyes of my friend Hannah, who was all ready to go in her factory-installed fur coat. So we went.

I did not enjoy the weather at all, but I was grateful that

I could go on another walk with my friend. She has already lasted well past the predicted time we were given, and who knows how many more chances we will have. I found myself shivering and worshiping. As we walked, I was miserable and happy at the same time. Having an attitude of gratitude can make that weird combo plate possible. You can choose gratitude even while going through the valley. Gratitude resets the motivation to live for God and trust Him in the darkness. Philip Yancey reminds us why it makes perfect sense in his wonderful book *What's So Amazing about Grace?*

> If we comprehend what Christ has done for us, then surely out of gratitude we will strive to live "worthy" of such great love. We will strive for holiness not to make God love us but because he already does.[4]

Develop an attitude of gratitude. It will change your daily routine. My new target for how to live was summed up by a sign I noticed recently.

"I wish I enjoyed *anything* as much as my dog enjoys *everything!*"

Hannah lives with that exuberant joy. I still struggle at times when things go wrong. But my friend is modeling a valuable lesson twice a day in front of her food bowl, grateful for every bite.

CHAPTER 12

BURY THE BONES OF BITTERNESS

To err is human, to forgive, canine.

~UNKNOWN

Journal Entry

*Today I got ready to join my bride at our local workout
facility. Hannah saw my T-shirt, workout shorts, and
running shoes, and her pooch processor whirred and
came up with one word:*
  WALK!
  *You would have thought I had thrown her toys in
the fireplace from the look she gave me as I left the
house without her. She went to the window and shot
me one more mournful expression to make sure I got the
message. Fast-forward one hour. Joni and I come back
in the house, and there is Hannah greeting us with a toy
in her mouth and unbridled joy.*
  *The sad-eyed and deeply betrayed canine of just one
hour ago was long forgotten. All was forgiven.*

Hannah is all about forgiveness. Dogs do have an amazing ability to look past loutish behavior from their human friends. English writer George Eliot noted this gift. "We long for an affection altogether ignorant of our faults. Heaven has accorded this to us in the uncritical canine attachment."

Let's take a little quiz to determine who loves you most in your home. Lock your spouse/significant other and your dog outside in the rain for thirty minutes. When you finally open the door, which one is glad to see you? (Disclaimer: *Cue fast-talking announcer.* This story is for illustration only and should not be tried with your actual spouse/significant other. Side effects may occur, including loss of sleeping arrangements.)

Forgiveness may be the most unnatural thing that God asks us to do. Our wounded hearts cry out for justice, fairness, and retribution. That is the American way! But Jesus comes along and says forgive. The amazing thing about God's infinite wisdom is that He knows our wiring. More than anything else, forgiveness is a gift provided for *our* healing and only secondarily for the other person.

Part of the process of healing relationships with the bipeds in our lives is to address old wounds that need to be buried and forgotten. When I found out that my mom's health was failing, I knew that I had to resolve some issues that had been buried in my heart. I could choose to address them now or wait and address them more painfully later, as I was reminded by this quote from the book *TrueFaced*. "We may try to ignore it or stuff it away, but though it may lie dormant for a while, unresolved sin is always buried alive."[1] And those things buried alive will surface at the most surprising and emotionally devastating times.

Mom grew up in an emotionally distant and demanding

family. She never heard the words "I love you," never was hugged or shown any kind of physical affection. Instead, appearance and performance were considered paramount qualities that she, in turn, emulated in the home I grew up in. Living in that environment, I always felt like I came up short, that I never accomplished enough or even was enough as a person. Even now I still have to fight thoughts of viewing myself as a "not enough" little boy when certain emotional stimuli are present. My dad loved me but adopted a peace-at-all-costs philosophy that only exacerbated my feelings of not being enough. The truth is that I made mistakes with my own boys. I did the best I could to break some of the negative chains of my family history, but I know I failed at times.

My mom had done the best she could with the hand dealt to her. But God in His grace asked me to remember my own sin and shortcomings as a parent and forgive her. She forgave me for unfair expectations I had of her that she could not realistically deliver. After that conversation, relief flooded my heart and soul.

Sometimes the act of forgiveness does go that smoothly, but often it does not. Sometimes the other party does not cooperate. Sometimes the offense is so heinous that reconciliation is not only unlikely, it is dangerous. Then what? Please understand that these are principles of forgiveness and reconciliation that God's Word gives us. God also gives us discernment through the Holy Spirit and through His community of believers. Your situation may require that community to support and provide wisdom. But I am sure about one thing. Forgiveness is critical to healing. How it looks will be as unique as your own story.

I marvel that Hannah simply does not hold onto bitterness and grudges. Perhaps dogs are God's exhibit A of how to live happily by not retrieving grudges. In fact, a grudge may be the only thing Hannah refuses to retrieve.

Researchers are discovering that there are physical effects linked to harboring bitterness and grudges. An article in *USA Today* tantalizingly titled, "Psychologists Now Know What Makes People Happy," reported the findings of University of Michigan professor Christopher Peterson. (For this native Buckeye to agree with a Michigan prof shows the potential of grace in our lives.) Peterson stated that *forgiveness is the behavior most strongly linked to happiness.* Sounds like something from the New Testament, doesn't it? The professor correctly noted, "It's the queen of all virtues, and probably the hardest to come by."[2]

Sadly, we have found that statement to be true in the faith community as well. Christians have not always been noticeably better than the general populace on the forgiveness front.

Jesus does not give us a lot of loopholes in the texts about forgiveness. How about this command from the Gospel of Luke as a squirm-inducing reminder of the need to forgive?

If another believer sins, rebuke that person; then if there is repentance, forgive. Even if that person wrongs you seven times a day and each time turns again and asks forgiveness, you must forgive.

LUKE 17:3-4

Seriously, Lord? Maybe I could manage once or twice, but doesn't continually forgiving make me a fool?

Isn't it interesting how we wrestle with God about what He really meant when it comes to our own responses? "Give me grace, but for heaven's sake don't ask me to give it!" The text seems pretty clear in all of the translations. There are no exceptions. And then the apostle Paul doubles down on the forgiveness challenge.

> Be kind to each other, tenderhearted, forgiving one another, just as God through Christ has forgiven you.
> EPHESIANS 4:32

That is a very tall order and one that is impossible to do without remembering how much I have been forgiven. If you say something nasty about me and ask for forgiveness, I will almost certainly grant it. If you do it again and ask forgiveness, I will probably forgive you. If you do the same thing again and ask forgiveness, I will most likely respond ungraciously and ask you to "prove" you are sorry.

Yet that illustration is exactly what I do in my relationship with God every day. I have asked Him to forgive the same sin dozens, even hundreds of times. Still His Word tells me I am forgiven and He loves me just the same as the first time I confessed that sin. That is how God has forgiven me through Christ. I should respond accordingly, forgiving each and every offense out of profound gratitude. Do you see any way around the obvious command to forgive? Me neither.

Bottom line: we are commanded to forgive as we have been forgiven. Forgiveness may well be the missing ingredient to the healing of most relationships. Forgive the one who wounded you. Forgive yourself and seek forgiveness if you are the one who wounded. Perhaps your efforts will not result in reconciliation. That is sad but ultimately okay. What if the other person does not deserve to be forgiven? Consider Jesus as He looked down in agony from the cross.

Jesus said, "Father, forgive them, for they don't know what they are doing." And the soldiers gambled for his clothes by throwing dice.

LUKE 23:34

I can say with complete confidence that I have not endured the level of wounds, betrayal, mocking, and abuse that Jesus experienced. Yet He could look at those evil perpetrators and ask His Father to forgive them. That gives me some perspective. Perhaps my situations are forgivable, with His help and only with His help.

I have spent a lot of unhappy moments not enjoying the freedom the Lord intended because I did not want to forgive someone who hurt me. I grieve to think of how I have stubbornly refused to forgive others for real and/or perceived slights over the years. I can imagine Jesus looking at me with sadness (not condemnation) because I have not fully comprehended the magnitude of the debt that has been erased from my account because of Him. I can hear Him saying, "Dave, when you choose to hold onto bitterness, you shortchange yourself on joy and peace." If I cannot forgive, I have forgotten or never comprehended how much I have been forgiven.

Hannah doesn't understand the complexity of relationships that we must deal with in our lives. She forgives me because she trusts me, which is a way of life for her. Maybe we can learn a lot from the smaller brains and bigger hearts of our canine friends.

• • •

I have had a chance to apply some of the lessons I have been learning. Years ago I was on my old stomping grounds in southern Ohio with one night left before heading back to

Texas. One of my standard activities in my hometown was to hang out with my best friend from high school, Bob Novak, to drink coffee, reminisce, and agree about how incredibly funny we thought we were. On that particular night I was tired and asked him for a rain check. A short time later Bob was killed in an accident.

For all these years I carried incredible guilt that I had missed my final chance to be with my friend. I heard the voices of condemnation. "Great friend you were. You were a little bit tired and you were too selfish to be a friend." I felt so ashamed that I had let him down.

Going through this process of burying the bones of bitterness has allowed me to forgive myself. Here is what I believe to be true. He knew I was his friend. He knew that I loved him and I knew he loved me. I am sure he thought nothing about me begging off on that night.

I forgave myself today. There was no wrong motive that night. I was just tired. I carried that guilt for way too many years.

The apostle Paul knew our tendency and even sad delight in beating ourselves up over issues like these. It hurt to lose my friend. It hurt that I didn't get a final time to laugh and share. But I believe now that my friend would not condemn me for one moment. Paul talks about no condemnation from an eternal perspective. It is the passage that contains a verse that has already played a role in this journey.

I have discovered this principle of life—that when I want to do what is right, I inevitably do what is wrong. I love God's law with all my heart. But there is another power within me that is at war with my mind. This power makes me a slave to the sin that is still within me. Oh, what a miserable person I am! Who will free me from this life that is dominated by sin and death? Thank God! The answer is in Jesus Christ our Lord. So you see how it is: In my mind I really want to obey God's law, but because of my sinful nature I am a slave to sin. *So now there is no condemnation for those who belong to Christ Jesus.* And because you belong to him, the power of the life-giving Spirit has freed you from the power of sin that leads to death.

ROMANS 7:21–8:2, EMPHASIS ADDED

No condemnation. None. Nada. Zip. What part of *no* do I not understand? Yet we have a hard time believing that truth. Surely there must be some condemnation from God. It doesn't make sense. I mean, look at how I blew it again. How can Jesus let me skate on that? Of course there are consequences to sin and bad decisions. But we need never compound that with shame and guilt that causes us to *hide from the One who can keep us from making another bad choice.*

Maybe this is one more way that our canine friends can be breathing role models of grace. Hannah could be the poster puppy for no condemnation. Nothing that I do causes her to abandon me. No selfish act on my part drives her away. She is incapable of condemnation. I can ignore Hannah. Snap at her. Refuse her nuzzles. And then when I call her name, she runs to me with the undignified abandon of the father to his prodigal son. What an example of forgiving grace!

Because we are God's beloved children, Jesus is incapable of condemning us. I know that those who fear that Christians will take advantage of grace push back against statements like that with varying levels of civility. Doug Kelly once mused that "If you want to make people mad, preach law. If you want to make them really, really mad preach grace."[3] Again, let me be clear. Sin has consequences, and they can be ugly. God allows those consequences to play out in order to teach us tough lessons. But I am convinced of this. He never condemns me, because condemnation is the antithesis of grace.

• • •

There are three men in my life whom I trust with everything about me. We call ourselves the Redwood Brothers based on a unique characteristic of California's redwood trees. The coastal redwoods have shallow root systems that extend over one hundred feet from the base, intertwining with the roots of other redwoods. This increases their stability during strong winds and floods. That describes the four of us. We are men who desire to follow Christ faithfully and love our wives and families well. Yet we, too, have shallow root systems, and we need the strength of one another as we go through strong winds and floods together.

A couple of years ago we got together to identify the two biggest lies we continued to believe about ourselves. We wrote them on rocks with a permanent ink marker and buried them in the desert location where we were meeting. There was power in physically burying those lies. I have been tempted to dig up those lies from time to time, but I remember how freeing it was to shovel dirt on them until I couldn't see them anymore.

I thought of that symbolic gesture today as I prayed about burying the bones of bitterness I have held onto for far too long. Hannah is a perfect role model of forgiveness, demonstrating the fruit of the Spirit more consistently than her master!

Here is Hannah's fruit of the Spirit scorecard.

- ☑ Love
- ☑ Joy
- ☑ Peace
- ☑ Patience
- ☑ Kindness
- ☑ Goodness
- ☑ Faithfulness

The only one she might need to spend some quiet time reflecting on is self-control, especially when a squirrel is nearby. That's okay. We all have things to work on.

I have joked that if you give me a congregation of Labradors and golden retrievers we will have a revival. Sure, the sniffing during fellowship might be awkward, but what a loving community that would be!

Hannah forgives the bad parts of me before I forgive myself.

That is a living, breathing illustration of how Jesus has already forgiven me even before I confess. In a small way, Hannah shows me what that kind of forgiveness looks like in a broken world.

CHAPTER 13

WELCOME WAGGIN'

Money will buy a pretty good dog, but it won't buy the wag of his tail.

~JOSH BILLINGS, PEN NAME OF HENRY WHEELER SHAW

Journal Entry

Hannah often goes with me on routine errand road trips. Today I could not take her and left her with sad eyes staring at me through the door as I drove off. About a mile down the road I realized that I had forgotten my phone, so I doubled back home. I had been gone about five minutes. Hannah greeted me like I had just returned from war. How can I possibly keep from smiling?

Hannah is a real-life illustration of one of my favorite Jerry Seinfeld stand-up bits. "Let's examine the dog mind: Every time you come home, he thinks it's amazing. He can't believe that you've accomplished this again. You walk in the door. The joy of it almost kills him. 'He's back again! It's that guy! It's that guy!'"[1]

Hannah has two very different daytime wake-up modes. When things are normal and everyone is home, she gets up slowly, takes a step, then stretches luxuriously. She takes another slow step, enjoys a final big stretch, and is good to go. Then there is the Code Red EGS (Emergency Greeting System), an urgent and frenetic mode that is triggered whenever one of Hannah's family members or friends returns after an absence. It doesn't matter how long a person has been gone—it could be two minutes or two weeks. The response is the same.

Right now, Hannah is sprawled on the couch, lying on her back with legs askew. Hopefully Joni's statute of limitations has expired for Hannah not to be on the furniture. Hannah and I will keep this between us for the moment.

Suddenly I hear the garage door opening. Joni's home. Hannah looks like she has been zapped by a 120-volt charge of electricity. The EGS has been fully activated. Hannah's legs start flailing as she scrambles up, looking like a fireman answering a five-alarm call. She darts around frantically looking for a toy. She cannot welcome someone without a ball or toy stuffed in her mouth—that would be a clear violation of Labrador protocol. *Hooray, my plush duck!* She grabs it and bolts to the door. The excitement intensifies and Hannah starts twirling with the toy firmly secure. Round and round she goes, seeming to be propelled by her wildly wagging tail. Her body pulsates in anticipation.

How can you not be touched by a response like that? A dog is a self-esteem booster shot every time you show up. In a world where honest affirmation is a currency seldom spent, your canine friend is a rare asset indeed. Feeling unloved? Your dog friend will shower affection on you. Feeling a little stupid? Humorist Dave Barry observed that your dog thinks you are a genius. "You can say any fool thing to a dog, and the dog will give you this look that says, '. . . You're RIGHT! I NEVER would have thought of that!'"[2] Even as I write these words, Hannah has primed the EGS by sleeping with one paw on a toy at the ready if the need arises.

Why do we love our dogs so much? We all desire to be accepted for who we really are. In my opinion, no creature pulls off that kind of acceptance better than a dog. It was a wise but anonymous writer who wrote, "I hope to be the kind of person my dog thinks I am." Your canine friend does not care a lick (pun possibly intended) about your income, looks, or status. All he or she cares about is being with you. That kind of genuine affirmation is healing.

All of us need that kind of balm when our self-esteem has been banged up, usually more times than most of us are willing to admit. Because some people are extremely needy, we tend to swing way too far on the affirmation needs pendulum to try and not be "that person." And yet, deep down, we hope someone notices and says something that encourages us in a healthy and loving way.

When Hannah was diagnosed with cancer, my behavior toward her subtly changed. If I had to go somewhere without her, I would walk over to my sleeping friend, lean over, and give her a friendly pat before leaving the room. I called her more often to come over for an ear rub, even in the midst of my work. I rarely passed by her without pausing to give her a little scratch on the head. I did not want to miss any chance to show her my affection.

Why does that mind-set have to be sparked by the prospect of loss? Shouldn't that be the default for all relationships? Why don't I unfailingly give my wife a little hug or love pat each time she's near? Why don't I make it a priority to give a friend an embrace? The act of a caring touch is a powerful gesture in any relationship. The problem is that most of us are too self-absorbed to even think of it.

Hannah is teaching me the stunning power of affirmation. What if I greeted Joni using Hannah's method? A few things might have to be adapted. I probably won't stuff a toy in my mouth, although there have been times when something stuffed in my sarcastic mouth would be appropriate. Here is how my Hannah-approved relationship dynamic might look when Joni comes home from work.

I drop what I am doing to greet Joni, genuinely excited to see her.

I show her physical affection without any ulterior motive.

I am completely interested in her.

I accept her mood, whatever it might be, without judgment.

I listen to her frustrations without demanding to know how she could feel that way or offering countless "solutions."

If she needs to talk, I am wholly present.

If she cannot meet my needs, I am not angry or withdrawn.

Think that behavior might develop some good relationship vibes with my bride? That is what Hannah provides me with every single day. I have often called her "furry Prozac" for her ability to soothe and calm my anxieties. I wasn't surprised to learn that a few minutes alone with a pet dog or cat might do more to help people's stress than talking about their troubles with their best friend or spouse.

"While the idea of a pet as social support may appear to some as a peculiar notion, our participants' responses to stress combined with their descriptions of the meaning of pets in their lives suggest to us that social support can indeed cross species,"[3] says Karen Allen, a research scientist and the lead author of a study in 2002.

I think it is pretty clear that our canine friends can "cross species" to lift our spirits with adoring affirmation. If you have not come from a family culture of affirmation (and many of us have not), then a pet's affection can be a big part of the healing process.

As I previously mentioned, my mom never displayed affection to me when I was growing up. Every Mother's Day I would struggle to find a card that expressed my love but didn't say more than I could honestly own.

When her health began to fail, I reflected on our relationship. It had not always been rosy, but I began to think of ways she had attempted to show her love. Although she could not say the words "I'm sorry," I always knew that when she baked a special pie or made my favorite dish she was offering her emotional equivalent. She struggled to express her devotion verbally but I was convinced that she would run into hell in a gasoline-soaked suit to protect me if necessary. I began to affirm her for the good things she gave me. "Mom, I always look forward to your bean soup and corn bread when I come home," I told her. It was true; I loved her bean soup. As silly as singing the praises of bean soup may have sounded to someone else, her face lit up when I recognized her love language.

"The boys love their jerseys. We will send you pictures." Her smile made me smile. As I continued to affirm the good things I saw in her, it opened doors in her heart and in mine.

We have enough people (plus Satan) to remind us of our shortcomings and failings. We need to look through the lens of grace to let people know what is good about them. How powerful is the process of affirming the good in those we love? Immeasurable.

By affirming my mom, I began to change my attitude toward her. Was it a coincidence that as my attitude changed she reached a point of being able to say "I love you" and "I'm sorry"?

If you are losing someone dear, I would encourage you to affirm that person, letting your loved one know the good things that you see in his or her life. If the relationship has been a challenge, perhaps you will need to be creative, but I believe in most cases you can find something admirable.

We should not be surprised that people respond positively when they are told how much they matter. More important, we matter to God. His Word is full of affirmation for those who choose to trust Him.

> To all who believed him and accepted him, he gave the right to become *children of God.*
>
> JOHN 1:12, EMPHASIS ADDED

> You are the ones *chosen by God,* chosen for the high calling of priestly work, *chosen to be a holy people, God's instruments to do his work and speak out for him,* to tell others of the night-and-day difference he made for you— from nothing to something, from rejected to accepted.
>
> I PETER 2:9-10, *The Message,* EMPHASIS ADDED

Even before he made the world, *God loved us and chose us in Christ to be holy and without fault in his eyes.*

EPHESIANS 1:4, EMPHASIS ADDED

We are God's masterpiece. He has created us anew in Christ Jesus, so we can do the good things he planned for us long ago.

EPHESIANS 2:10, EMPHASIS ADDED

No longer do I call you servants, for the servant does not know what his master is doing; but *I have called you friends*, for all that I have heard from my Father I have made known to you.

JOHN 15:15, ESV, EMPHASIS ADDED

Jesus calls me His friend. Even when those around you are failing to fill up your affirmation bucket, you can still go to Scripture and find out how God feels about you. Is there a more important affirmation than that? When you believe that your heavenly Father recognizes your worth, it gets easier to find things to affirm in others. How can I suffer from a poor self-image if this is true? Jesus calls me *friend*, for goodness' sake!

Don't miss a chance to affirm others. Be intentional, making it a way of life. Hannah has me enrolled in intensive affirmation training. Every time my canine instructor sees me, she treats me like the most important person in the world. Her exuberance never fails to warm my heart. As for me, I can't promise I will shake and do pirouettes when I see a person I love. But I will do my best to say something to make his or her day.

CHAPTER 14

ONLY THE GOOD DIE YOUNG?

If you have a dog, you will most likely outlive it; to get a dog is to open yourself to profound joy and, prospectively, to equally profound sadness.

~MARJORIE GARBER

Journal Entry

*Today I heard Billy Joel singing that only the good die
young. I suspect the good and bad die with about the
same mortality rates. The difference is we care so much
more about the good people and animals who have
touched our lives. Today I was grateful to welcome
my friend to day number 315 in her journey. She has
lived far beyond my expectations from that first painful
jolt of bad news. The effects of her disease are slowly
beginning to appear, but she still is living happily "in
the moment" each day. I have had more time to prepare
than I suspected. Part of that lesson is accepting that
her life both pre-diagnosis and post-diagnosis has been*

a gift. But I know that day is coming when I must say
good-bye.

Joni and I know we are living on God-given grace time
with our friend Hannah. We monitor her health closely,
watching for anything that seems unusual, concerned when
she seems out of sorts.

Today I was on the road (again) when I got a call from
Joni. "Hannah's acting funny," she said. "She hasn't eaten
today and seems sluggish. I can't even get her to play." My
mind went straight to the worst-case scenario and tears filled
my eyes.

"I'm going to take her to the vet," Joni said. "I will call
you back."

A couple of restless hours went by. When the phone
finally rang, I was eager to answer it and also afraid.

"Hey," I said weakly. Even that was difficult to say.

"Hannah just has an infection. The doctor gave her some
antibiotics and she is already perking up."

I exhaled. *Thank You, Lord, for more precious days with our*
friend. I renewed my resolution to live fully in every moment
with her.

• • •

There is a story that has circulated through cyberspace for
years about a young boy who is in the examining room with a
veterinarian, saying a final good-bye to the family pet. Trying
to console the boy, the vet says, "It's sad that animals don't
live as long as their human friends." There is a moment of
silence and then the boy pipes up, "I know why."

"You do?" the vet replies.

"Sure. People are born so that they can learn how to live

a good life—like loving everybody all the time and being nice, right?" The vet nods as the boy continues, "Well, dogs already know how to do that, so they don't have to stay as long."

That would certainly explain why Hannah didn't need to hit the high end of her breed life expectancy. She had mastered her "grace" skills early.

The truth is that no creature knows how many days are allotted to him or her. When we heard the news about Hannah, my first reaction was that she was "too young" for such a hideous prognosis. The reality was that it wasn't unusual for her age and breed. I was the one who decided she was way too young.

Sir Walter Scott celebrated dogs in his writings as well as in his life. He, too, grew very close to his canine friends. "I have sometimes thought of the final cause of dogs having such short lives, and I am quite satisfied it is in compassion to the human race; for if we suffer so much in losing a dog after an acquaintance of ten or twelve years, what would it be if they were to live double that time?"[1] I had never considered that a dog's shorter life span was a gift of grace.

Because of Hannah's active, athletic lifestyle I just assumed she would exceed the average life span by many years, slowing down as she reached doggie old age. Yet none of us are guaranteed that simply because we are active or eat healthy or are good people (or puppies), we will live well into our sunset years.

This journey with Hannah has prompted me to begin examining my own fears about dying. The irony is that I could have suffered a heart attack or been killed in an accident before Hannah's time was over. Sportscaster Dan Patrick had a classic rejoinder along those lines when he described an injured athlete. "He's listed as day to day, but then again, aren't we all?"[2] I circled back around to Dr. Woolley's statement after Hannah's surgery: "Hannah has no fear of death, so she lives in the moment."

One of the amazing things about these special friends is how they accept what each day gives. If Hannah wakes up feeling a little pain, she still finds a way to wag her tail and smile a doggy smile. When we had to take Hannah to the vet to have a small tumor aspirated, she was understandably scared of the needle. I bet it stung. But the vet tech knew exactly what to do during the procedure—scratching Hannah's ears the whole time while Hannah "said" thanks with her wagging tail. Even in that scary moment she found a way to express joy.

She has taught me so much about moment-to-moment joy. I write this as a Christian who believes that I have become a child of God because of my faith in Jesus. I believe I have a spot reserved in eternity with Him. I believe (intellectually) the Scripture passage that Jesus has gone to prepare a place for me.[3] And yet, forcing myself to consider death made me wonder if I really lived as if I truly believed all those things.

Honestly, I didn't like my conclusion. I believe in heaven, but only as a last resort. I don't mean that to be flippant. I have come to the realization that I did not completely comprehend the hope of eternity.

When I was a young man, I compiled a mental bucket list of things that I hoped would happen before I died. I wanted to get married and have children. When that was checked off, I added grandchildren and other things to the list. All the items on my list of things hoped for before I entered heaven were good things. But how I viewed those things versus eternity showed me that I did not have a good theology of what life after death means. Those things were not just desires. They were very often idols, the "good things that became ultimate things."

German pastor Dietrich Bonhoeffer, who died at the hands of the Nazis in World War II for standing up for what he knew was true, was fearless about death.

> Why are we so afraid when we think about death? . . . Death is only dreadful for those who live in dread and fear of it. Death is not wild and terrible, if only we can be still and hold fast to God's Word. Death is not bitter, if we have not become bitter ourselves. Death is grace, the greatest gift of grace that God gives to people who believe in him. Death is mild, death is sweet and gentle; it beckons to us with heavenly power, if only we realize that it is the gateway to our homeland, the tabernacle of joy, the everlasting kingdom of peace.[4]

Wow. Do I believe that? That was an eye-opening, heart-wrenching indictment of how shallow my faith really has been regarding eternity. Death is not the final chapter of our lives; it's simply the prologue to joy and peace. Have I ever thought of death as God's greatest gift of grace? Hardly. Yet that is the reality of our faith if we believe the gospel is true.

Hannah's journey has radically changed my mind-set. If I knew I were to die soon, I would be sad that I would miss sweet time with my bride, my children and grandchildren, and my friends. I would hope that a few of them would miss me. But with renewed faith and hope, I would spend time thinking of what lies ahead.

One of my favorite authors, Randy Alcorn, gets right to the point.

Many Christians dread the thought of leaving this
world. Why? Because so many have stored up their
treasures on earth, not in heaven. Each day brings
us closer to death. If your treasures are on earth,
that means each day brings you closer to losing your
treasures.[5]

My treasures are in heaven or, I pray, going to be there.
My dad, my mom, my nephew, Dean, and my beloved
grandmother are among the many people who have gone
ahead of me and whom I long to see there. My daughter,
Katie, is waiting for me. Perhaps my sense of restlessness is
not because I'm bored with my life, but something much
deeper, as C. S. Lewis proposed. "If I find in myself a desire
which no experience in this world can satisfy, the most prob-
able explanation is that I was made for another world."[6]

The thought of reunions made me think of several touch-
ing videos showing soldiers returning from deployment and
being greeted by their dogs. One of my favorites is a boxer
named Chuck that goes berserk when he's reunited with
his returning friend.[7] Even an adjective as strong as *berserk*
does not fully communicate the joy this dog showed to his
long-absent master.

It brought to mind an experience last year from my job
with the Texas Rangers that might offer a glimpse of my
heavenly reunion someday. It was a sports director's dream
moment. The Rangers had a few "walk-off" wins last season,
scoring the winning run in the last at bat at home. When a
game is over, both teams walk off the field but with very different body languages.

In this particular game against the Los Angeles Angels,
the score was all tied up in the bottom of the ninth with two

outs on the board. Rangers' catcher Geovany Soto was at the plate. I was with my crew in a portable television studio built into a truck trailer. The TV truck features dozens of monitors filled with camera shots, graphics, and replay sources. I orchestrate the broadcast from my seat in front of a huge bank of camera monitors, communicating by headset to camera operators where we are going next. I select a shot from the monitors in front of me, and the technical director pushes a button that puts it "on the air," instantaneously sending it into your home. When the action is fast and furious, it all seems chaotic, but each person has his or her assignment and it all comes together in a frenzied symphony of teamwork.

I scan the monitors, focusing on Soto's intense concentration. The Angels' closer is trying to send a tie game into extra innings. The Rangers players are hanging on the dugout rail, hoping that Soto will come through. The count goes full. Two outs. And then it happens. The ball is driven deep to left field. The Rangers players start to jump up and down as the ball heads toward the stands, then leaves the park. Pandemonium ensues inside the park, and my production crew explodes in excitement too. But we have a job to do to bring the images home to our fans.

Rangers players Elvis Andrus and Adrian Beltre and others leap the rail and sprint toward home plate to greet the hero of the moment. Soto rounds third, flips his helmet in the air with joy, and sprints toward a throng of teammates encircling home plate. They are smiling and waiting anxiously for Soto to get "home" so they can celebrate. As he nears home plate, Soto makes a gigantic leap and disappears into the dogpile of teammates. What a picture. That is the drama of sports. Even the apostle Paul used sports as an analogy for spiritual things.

I do everything to spread the Good News and share in its blessings. Don't you realize that in a race everyone runs, but only one person gets the prize? So run to win! All athletes are disciplined in their training. They do it to win a prize that will fade away, but we do it for an eternal prize.

I CORINTHIANS 9:23-25

I reflected on that passage and the thrilling finish of that Rangers-Angels game. As electrifying as it was, that victory is nothing compared to holding the eternal prize that will not fade away when I finish this earthly race. I began to imagine my heavenly homecoming and how it might resemble that "walk-off" moment. I saw myself rounding third and heading toward all of the loved ones who had gone ahead, the joy of their faces compelling me to run faster. I jumped into a dogpile of dear friends and family who had shared my journey. When I finally emerged from the ecstatic group, I saw Jesus. He hugged me warmly. I was safe at home.

Hannah has given me a little glimpse of my future heavenly reception. When I walk through my front door in a foul humor and am greeted with no judgment or condemnation, I receive a little taste of heavenly grace. Hannah only sees what is good about me, and she welcomes me with unconditional love. God forgets my sin and sees only what is good about me, and on those days when my attitude is less than heavenly, He still sees the redeeming face of Jesus. There is no condemnation in Him. If we can experience a taste of that on this planet, how sweet it will be to finally make it home.

CHAPTER 15

GOOD-BYE

Not the least hard thing to bear when they go from us, these quiet friends,
is that they carry away with them so many years of our own lives.

~JOHN GALSWORTHY

Journal Entry

Today I had to catch a late afternoon charter flight with the Texas Rangers for the next road trip. I didn't want to leave the house because Hannah is showing signs that the end is nearing. I lay on the floor with her much of the afternoon, stroking her and giving back to her the comfort she so often gave to me. I had a difficult time leaving, and I nearly missed the flight. The team personnel weren't happy with me, but I decided to just stay quiet rather than explain why I was late. What could I say? I had to squeeze out every second I could with my friend.

I was pretty sure when I left the house today that I would not see Hannah again. This morning I had helped her into our pool, and in spite of her waning strength, she was eager to get in the cool water. I joined her and we had what I suspected would be our last swim. She enjoyed the pool so much, even now at the end. I'm sure the water helped relieve her aching joints as she slowly dog-paddled in a circle. Her body was failing, but she still had the spirit of a puppy as she moved.

As I watched Hannah, I realized she was giving me her final lesson: never miss a moment of joy in the journey. These last weeks, she slept more and undoubtedly was in pain, but she still could muster a friendly wag and enjoy a moment. She simply accepted that this is how she felt on any given day. No feeling sorry for herself or pity parties. Hannah has lived, truly lived, until she can live no more. What an example from my faithful friend!

I hoped against hope that my farewell today would not be for good. But I knew that she was weary and it was time.

Four days later Joni called to give me an update. "Hannah won't eat and I have to help her outside. She can't even get up from her bed. I don't want to leave her alone but I'm needed at work, so I'll see if Mike and Debbie can check on Hannah." Mike and Debbie Johnston are our neighbors and they dearly loved Hannah. The feeling was mutual.

I called Mike later that morning. I knew what he was going to say before he said a word, but Mike's response still punched me in the heart. "She is not doing well." Mike and Debbie stayed at our house all morning with Hannah, lying beside her on the floor, gently petting and talking to her until Joni arrived home. When Mike volunteered to accompany Joni to the vet, she took him up on his gracious offer. She didn't want to do this alone.

Mike gently carried Hannah to our car. Our regular veterinarian, Dr. Julie Stanek, who had cared for Hannah since she was a puppy, was waiting for Joni and Mike at the clinic. Could there be one more miracle she could offer Hannah?

When Dr. Stanek saw Hannah, she knew it was indeed time. Again, a compassionate and caring vet made a difference. She gave Joni some time with Hannah to say good-bye. Tears were shed all around as Hannah peacefully passed out of her pain.

Even though I knew for months that this day was coming, I wasn't prepared for how hard the news hit me. I don't cry easily, but every time I thought of Hannah guilt kicked in and the tears started. *I'm so sorry that I couldn't be there, my friend, to provide the strength and comfort that you selflessly gave me for eleven years.* Joni said good-bye for both of us; we were thankful that we were able to help Hannah die with dignity and grace.

From the day we brought her home from the surgery to the day that she died, we had Hannah for 499 days. What a gift! Even in my deep sorrow, I was grateful for the extra time. "Thank you, God, for bringing Hannah into my life. She has been a daily blessing to me and so many others."

When a beloved pet dies, the question is often raised, Do you think we will be reunited with our pets in heaven? Job wrote that "the soul of every living thing is in the hand of God" (Job 12:10, TLB). I love what Reverend Billy Graham said: "Heaven will be a place of perfect happiness for us— and if we need animals around us to make our happiness complete, then you can be sure God will have them there."[1]

I agree.

It reminds me of one of my favorite *Frank and Ernest* comic strips. A man is standing at the gate of heaven, ready to be checked in by St. Peter, who quips, "If you don't mind throwing tennis balls for eternity, I do have an opening in doggie heaven."

Hannah's joyous paw prints were deeply engraved on my heart, which made me sad. I thought I had prepared well through my journaling, but I couldn't accept that she was gone. Perhaps I found it more difficult because I had been on the road and couldn't be with her when she died. Perhaps it was simply my tendency to stuff feelings deep down in my heart and cover them over with vigorous activity and denial rather than face them.

For several weeks after Hannah died, I was depressed. I was melancholy and couldn't muster any energy. I became almost robotic in my actions, doing what I could to get through each day. Then I had an idea. A new dog! I thought bringing home a puppy would help pull me out of the doldrums. Joni wisely put a stop to that. "You're rushing," she counseled me. "You're not ready for another dog. You haven't fully grieved for Hannah yet." I didn't like that answer.

A few nights later I sat alone in my favorite chair after Joni fell asleep. *She's really gone.* I was overcome with loneliness, and in the stillness I finally released my sorrow, weeping without shame. *My dear friend is gone.* After that moment of emotional honesty I began to really heal. Hannah's lesson was sinking in: I needed to embrace joy, too.

• • •

Joni had had her opportunity to say good-bye. Now it was my turn to bid farewell, doing something Hannah and I enjoyed doing together for eleven years.

On a January morning I went to the cabinet and pulled out the wooden box that contained Hannah's ashes. I put on my walking clothes, remembering how Hannah would always shake with excitement when she realized what was coming next. I filled a small plastic baggie with some of the ashes, and Hannah and I set out for our final walk.

As I walked, I prayed out loud. "Thank you, God, for Hannah's eleven years of faithful friendship. You knew that she was going to be the perfect companion to walk with me through Joni's cancer. Some might say that Hannah came into our lives unexpectedly, but I know that You planned all this. It was a perfect plan with a wonderful dog." When we got to Hannah's favorite park, I couldn't help but feel her presence with me.

I walked to the back side of the park where Hannah would run in freedom and joy, and I scattered some of her ashes there. I tossed a little by the tree that the squirrels scrambled up to escape her mad dashes. I imagined her saying to them with a smile, "I'm still around." I let the wind take some ashes as I listened on my iPhone to "Tribute to a Dog," Walter Brennan's musical rendition of George Graham Vest's iconic speech, "Tribute to the Dog."

The one absolutely unselfish friend that man can have in this selfish world, the one that never deserts him, the one that never proves ungrateful or treacherous is his dog. A man's dog stands by him in prosperity and in poverty, in health and in sickness. He will sleep on the cold ground, where the wintry winds blow and the snow drives fiercely, if only he may be near his master's side. He will kiss the hand that has no food to offer. He will lick the wounds and sores that come in encounters with the roughness of the world. He guards the sleep of his pauper master as if he were a prince. When all other friends desert, he remains. When riches take wings, and reputation falls to pieces, he is as constant in his love as the sun in its journey through the heavens.[2]

"I'm so grateful, God. So very grateful." As I wiped the tears from my eyes, I headed back home. I spread some of Hannah's remains in the backyard where we played catch and fetch for countless hours. I took a tennis ball and threw it into the pool, anointing it with a few ashes. It just seemed appropriate.

God gave us a sunny and very windy day for that last walk. I gathered the final handful of Hannah's ashes and tossed them into the air. The wind caught the fine particles and whisked them upward. Her memory soared to the heavens, a fitting send-off.

Hannah's journey has changed me. I am more aware of living fully in each moment. I try to live in the freedom of God's grace. I am accepting with gratitude what each day brings me. I try to find joy even when I don't feel at my best. Hannah's graceful and uncomplaining acceptance of pain, and ultimately death, challenges me to become bolder than I have ever been. I want to echo Charles de Foucauld's words that "the one thing we owe absolutely to God is never to be afraid of anything." If we trust that God is who He says He is, we should never be afraid. I still fall short of that goal, but I am getting closer to that place of dependent trust.

There is a story told of a man close to death who expressed his fear of the end to his doctor. "Please, doctor, tell me what lies on the other side," the man said.

"I don't know," the doctor replied quietly.

"You don't know? But you're a Christian. How can you not know what is on the other side?"

The doctor's hand rested on the doorknob of the examination room; on the other side of the door the men could hear scratching and whining. When the doctor opened the door, a dog sprang into the room and nearly knocked him over with boundless happiness.

Turning to the patient, the doctor said, "My dog's never been in this room before. He didn't know what was inside, except for one thing. He knew that his master was here. When I opened the door, he leaped in without fear. The same is true for us. I don't know what is on the other side of death, but I do know one thing. I know my Master is there, and that is enough."

That is enough for me, too. I will embrace joy on this earth and look forward to endless joy in heaven because I know my Master is on the other side.

CHAPTER 16

FORGETTING HER NAME

*Whoever declared that love at first sight doesn't exist has never
witnessed the purity of a puppy or looked deep into a puppy's eyes.*

~ELIZABETH PARKER, *PAW PRINTS IN THE SAND*

JOURNAL ENTRY

I was wasting time on Facebook earlier this month when I noticed this post from a friend who provides temporary housing for rescued dogs seeking a forever home.

MEET SAVANNAH OUR NEW FOSTER.

That simple little bit of text would not have caused me to linger. But the photo that was with it—[the one on page 147]—caused me to stop in my tracks.

I couldn't take my eyes off those amazing eyes. I found out a little bit about the dog from my friend, so Joni and I decided to meet Savannah. No doubt you already know the rest of the story. Welcome to my new mentor.

We brought Savannah home for a trial run on Sunday, January 27, 2014. The pet adoption agency requests that prospective owners spend a couple of weeks with a dog before making a final decision, to make sure it's a good fit. From the minute she walked through the front door, Savannah was both curious and cautious. Obviously, she detected another dog's scent even though Hannah had been gone for months. Joni and I had a pile of new toys waiting for Savannah, as well as a new crate for her to relax and sleep in.

Our house guest was friendly but not overly affectionate. We figured that was due to the chaotic and uncertain events she had already experienced in her life. Savannah had been found running loose about forty-five miles north of our city, with a nasty gash on her hind leg. It was healed, although she had a permanent scar to remind us of her injury.

After the two weeks were up, we filled out the paperwork and arranged a final in-home visit so the agency was convinced we were "worthy" parents. (I'm glad they didn't use our boys as references.) What were the odds that Savannah would wind up with us? In keeping with the great Burchett family tradition, our new puppy match happened while we were making other plans.

All of the Burchett dogs have been either rescued or adopted. Our eldest son, Matt, and his wife, Holly, adopted their golden retriever friend, Bailey, in Nashville when they were first married. Hannah's friend, Sadie, found her forever home with middle son, Scott, and his wife, Caroline, before their two children arrived. One day when our youngest son, Brett, was driving in Waco, he spotted five puppies running along the road. He stopped to round up the pack, but only managed to catch one. It was love at first sight, and Brett named him Trigger. A few days later, Brett took the pup to a veterinary clinic for a checkup, where they discovered Trigger had the often deadly parvovirus. I could hear the sadness in Brett's voice when he called with the news. "At least he knew he was loved," he said with a quivering voice. There was never a doubt after that comment that I would reach into my wallet to cover the hospital stay. For the next ten days, Trigger was on an IV that saved his life. Today he is thriving as Brett's best buddy. As you can see, we know a thing or two about doggie adoption in our family.

The word *adoption* is one that the apostle Paul included in his letters to the early churches. In Romans he uses the example to powerfully illustrate how God views us.

> All who are led by the Spirit of God are children of God. So you have not received a spirit that makes you fearful slaves. Instead, you received God's Spirit when *he adopted you as his own children.* Now we call him, "Abba, Father." For his Spirit joins with our spirit to affirm that we are God's children. And since we are his children, *we are his heirs.* In fact, together with Christ we are heirs of God's glory. But if we are to share his glory, we must also share his suffering.
>
> ROMANS 8:14-17, EMPHASIS ADDED

Paul knew his Roman audience well, referencing their custom of adoption. In that culture you didn't have to be born into a family to be an heir; an outsider could be adopted into the family and receive the benefits of a blood relative. Adoption was meant to preserve the family, and there were no age restrictions—the adoptee could be a child or an adult. In each case, the adoptee's debts and obligations were erased, and the adoptee received a new identity.

That was our first order of business with our new canine friend Savannah. Her foster name "Savannah" was just too close to Hannah, so we began brainstorming other possibilities. Joni and I have a friend named Maggie who greets everyone with a smile and a cheerful, "Happy Day!" That seemed to match the personality of our adoptee, so with our friend's amused permission, we settled on Maggie.

There was only one problem with the new moniker. Our puppy would not respond to her new name. It wasn't unexpected. After all, she had been dubbed Savannah by the adoption center. Perhaps she had a different name before she found herself lost in the Texas countryside. Now we were trying to saddle her with a third name in less than a year of life. No wonder she was confused!

We concentrated on teaching the puppy her new name. "Maggie, come!" We gave her treats when she came when called and praised her profusely. We did all the things the dog training websites suggest to introduce a rescued puppy into a new environment. No matter what we tried, Maggie seemed to choose if, and when, she would respond to her name. It was frustrating to see her look in our direction when we called her and, a moment later, wander off with apparent disinterest.

Later I realized I had just learned my first lesson from my new mentor. I do the same thing with God. I was given a new name when I put my faith in Jesus as my Savior. My new identity, mentioned several times in the New Testament, is "child of God."

> To all who believed him and accepted him, he gave the right to become *children of God*.
> JOHN 1:12-13, EMPHASIS ADDED

If you live by [your sinful nature's] dictates, you will die. But if through the power of the Spirit you put to death the deeds of your sinful nature, you will live. For all who are led by the Spirit of God are *children of God*.

So you have not received a spirit that makes you fearful slaves. Instead, you received God's Spirit when he adopted you as *his own children*. Now we call him, "Abba, Father."

ROMANS 8:13-15, EMPHASIS ADDED

You are all *children of God* through faith in Christ Jesus.

GALATIANS 3:26, EMPHASIS ADDED

Because we are his *children*, God has sent the Spirit of his Son into our hearts, prompting us to call out, "Abba, Father."

GALATIANS 4:6, EMPHASIS ADDED

Everyone who believes that Jesus is the Christ has become a *child of God*. And everyone who loves the Father loves his *children*, too.

1 JOHN 5:1, EMPHASIS ADDED

So who am I? Expatriated Buckeye? TV sports director? Author of a modestly successful book? Husband of Joni? Father of three outstanding young men? Ridiculously proud grandfather? Member of Costco? All those things define me to some degree. But the one thing that is true about me that I find almost impossible to comprehend is that I am *a child of God*. Just like Maggie, sometimes I answer to my new name and sometimes I just wander off thinking, *You must not be talking about me.*

There is power in believing in a name. Many years ago, for

reasons I still don't understand, I was cast as the lead in our high school senior musical. I had never acted and was not a trained singer. And yet that stellar résumé somehow landed me the role as Don Quixote in *Man of La Mancha*. Go figure. The play is based on Miguel de Cervantes's seventeenth-century novel *Don Quixote*. The drama unfolds as a play within a play, performed by Cervantes and his fellow prisoners as he awaits a hearing with the Spanish Inquisition. Cervantes takes on the character of "mad knight" Don Quixote.

It was fun and challenging to learn page after page of dialogue as well as doing my best not to mess up "The Impossible Dream." I enjoyed transforming into an old man on stage and donning the armor of the knight errant.

As I became immersed in the character of Quixote, I began to understand that the gentle and naive protagonist saw the world through eyes of grace. He perceived what people can become and not what they are at the moment. When he meets a prostitute named Aldonza, Quixote sees her as a lady, treats her with respect, and gives her a new name—Dulcinea.

Aldonza's reaction? She lashes out with fury and hatred as all her past junk pours out. Aldonza agonizes that her mother doesn't know which of her many lovers might be Aldonza's father. She rages about men who have used, abused, and abandoned her. And now this man calls her a "lady" and gives her a new name and identity. Aldonza hates what she has become, but even more she hates the fear of believing she could change and possibly face another crushing disappointment. At least her identity in a questionable vocation is familiar. And yet Don Quixote sees her as a soul created with value who can be redeemed.

Gradually, Aldonza understands that Quixote is genuine, and she begins to believe what the old man says is true about her, that she does have value. When the "Quixotic" world of the man of La Mancha is destroyed and he draws his final breath, Sancho Panza, the faithful squire, addresses the grieving woman as Aldonza.

She gently corrects him. "My name is Dulcinea."

Her identity has been changed by an agent of grace.

That's what happens to those who place their trust in Christ. God gives us a new identity and He calls us by a new name.

His child.

We also tend to fight back and remind God of what we used to be and all that is wrong about us now. But Jesus patiently reminds us of our new identity. He tells us that we have been changed. That our spiritual DNA has been rewritten. That we are a new creation in Him. That we are holy. Saints. When we believe what Jesus says is true about us, it will change how we live our lives.

A righteous and beloved child of God. That is not an "impossible dream," but a theological truth.

I am a flawless child of God. Not because of anything I have done, am doing, or will ever do. It is because of what Jesus did for me on the cross. Whenever I start wavering, I need to pause and remember my name.

Maggie will learn her name with repetition and praise and reward. We are making real progress. Our dog trainer gave us a great tip. "Never use her name for shaming or punishment. When you call Maggie, she should expect to play, get a treat, or to be loved. Every time she hears 'Maggie' it should be a party."

I love that image for my journey with Jesus. When He calls my name, it is a party of grace, not of shaming or punishment. I am His beloved child. When He calls my name, it is for my good.

Dave Burchett, aka "child of God." That has a nice ring to it.

CHAPTER 17

THE IMPACT OF OUR STORY

*Saving one dog will not change the world, but surely
for that one dog, the world will change forever.*

~KAREN DAVISON

Journal Entry

For the first two weeks Maggie was pretty well behaved. But now she is showing some decidedly less attractive sides to her personality. She is independent. She is stubborn. She is affectionate only when she wants to be affectionate. She acts out on occasion. She chews things that are not approved for that activity. I am finding out that a "honeymoon" period is pretty common for rescue dogs. That was not mentioned in the brochure. Now that the honeymoon is over, I guess we get down to the challenge of making this relationship work.

I wish we knew more of Maggie's backstory. We found out from the veterinarian's report that Maggie had a fresh gash on her leg when she was rescued near Van Alstyne, Texas. The exam showed that she was visibly undernourished and tested positive for hookworms. Everything else was a mystery. Was she wanted and ran away? Was she unwanted and abandoned to fend for herself? Was she treated poorly? Had she been socialized with other animals and people? The details of her story—who, what, where, when, why—surely have influenced her behavior.

Maggie's biggest issue has been trust. I certainly get that. She was captured, kenneled, and then fostered. If I had been bounced around as a child, I would have trust issues. Oh, wait— I didn't experience any of that, and I still have trust issues.

Of course, Maggie isn't a unique case. Many rescued dogs suffer from behavioral baggage. Some have severe separation anxiety that may have started when the pups were taken from their mother too early. If a dog has fended for itself, it can become dangerously territorial over food and possessions. When a dog flinches or cowers at the gentlest human touch, it breaks my heart.

Each day, I tried to read Maggie's expressions and body language. Did she think we were just one more way station on her sad journey? She seemed appreciative of everything we gave her, yet she was still wary. Her personality was friendly at times, but then she'd become withdrawn and want to hide. She would accept affection but she rarely initiated it. The message she was sending was "It's okay. I can make it on my own."

Those survival skills made Maggie extremely sneaky. We would lose track of her for a moment and then find her counter surfing for treats or chewing on the dining room chairs. We would turn our backs and she would be into something. I have to admit that I was impressed that such a large dog could be stealthy; Maggie had figured it out. I would have to be exceedingly patient, kind, and consistent to win her trust. We sacrificed three dining room chairs during the trust-building phase of our relationship. At least Maggie intuitively chose furniture we had planned to replace soon anyway. Maybe she was really making a decorating statement more than acting out.

As I spent more time trying to understand Maggie's reactions and fears, I became convicted as I examined my own behavior toward others. Way too often I lack patience or am less than kind to the humans I encounter on my journey. I am quick to judge and quick to condemn without knowing what baggage in their lives might be contributing to their actions. Why am I so prone to do that? Charles Spurgeon offered this incredibly irritating thought: "None are more unjust in their judgments of others than those who have a high opinion of themselves." Ouch. Guilty as charged.

I fall into that trap when I forget who I am. I am a desperate sinner saved by grace.[1] I am the Prodigal who decided to sever the family ties, then came crawling back for mercy.[2] I am the Prodigal's older brother who felt superior to his wayward sibling because he did all the "right" things.[3] I am the field worker who showed up early and expected to be paid more than those who had been hired later in the day.[4] I am the follower of Jesus who conveniently got lost in the crowd when the going got too tough, the person who vowed to never back down and yet denies Him over and over by my words and actions.

Inexplicably, at the same time, I am beloved by God because Jesus died for me. I am adopted, sealed, and redeemed.[5] I am a friend of God.[6] I am forgiven. God loves me because of the finished work of His Son Jesus, and on my worst day He sees Jesus in me.[7]

When I forget who I am, I become a judging machine. I judge a person's appearance and position without taking the time to learn anything about him or her. Sometimes I catch myself in the act, which is disheartening. The country group Sawyer Brown sings about the danger of a rush to judgment in their powerfully convicting song, "They Don't Understand." The lyrics remind me that someone who might be acting angrily or sullenly toward me might be dealing with some unspoken personal tragedy that is sending him or her into an emotional free fall.

I witnessed this when I was driving from one of Joni's first doctor appointments after her breast cancer diagnosis. We had met at the doctor's office to hear what treatment options we faced and what our journey would look like for the next year. It was overwhelming to take it all in. Joni and I had driven separately, so when we left the doctor's office, I followed her. She was distracted (imagine that) and missed her turn, so she continued on to the next side street where she could turn left, then double back. There was no traffic light at that street, so Joni temporarily blocked the left lane. A guy behind her laid on his horn and started gesturing. I remember thinking, *This guy is not a quality human being* (or words to that effect). *Would it make a difference in the attitude of this, uhhh, not really nice driver if he knew what was going through my wife's mind? I'd be happy to let him know.* No, he was busy worrying about his thirty-second delay while Joni was thinking about her health, her family, her job, and maybe her life.

I was furious with this selfish stranger. But the truth is I am that man too. A man who is capable of doing nearly everything that I get angry about with others. And yet I am always humbled that somehow God is patient with me as I work to become less like me and more like Him.[8]

The tragedy is that the world most often perceives the Christian community as being judgmental rather than loving. The Barna Research Group surveyed people born between 1965 and 2002. Eighty-seven percent said the term *judgmental* accurately describes present-day Christianity.[9]

When Jesus was teaching in the Temple, He addressed those who condemned the healing of a man on the Sabbath. "Do not judge according to external appearance, but judge with proper judgment" (John 7:24, NET). I also like how it's worded in the New Living Translation. "Look beneath the surface so you can judge correctly."

I am taking that advice on the road this week. As I walk the streets of San Francisco, I am intentionally monitoring my reactions to those I encounter. My grade so far? Failing.

Even as I am consciously aware of my thoughts, I still smugly criticize bad hair and bad looks. I make value judgments about people without the slightest idea of their stories or hearts. How arrogant of me to look through any other lens than a lens of grace.

How much damage has been done in the name of Christ by well-meaning or just mean churchgoers? How much damage have I done with careless judgments and comments? Has someone rejected Christ because of how I represented Him? *The Message* frames a familiar passage in Romans that we should reread often. The apostle Paul gets right to the point about how we judge "those people," the people who don't acknowledge God.

> Those people are on a dark spiral downward. But if you think that leaves you on the high ground where you

can point your finger at others, think again. *Every time you criticize someone, you condemn yourself.* It takes one to know one. Judgmental criticism of others is a well-known way of escaping detection in your own crimes and misdemeanors. *But God isn't so easily diverted. He sees right through all such smoke screens and holds you to what you've done.* You didn't think, did you, that just by pointing your finger at others you would distract God from seeing all your misdoings and from coming down on you hard? Or did you think that because he's such a nice God, he'd let you off the hook? Better think this one through from the beginning. God is kind, but he's not soft. In kindness he takes us firmly by the hand and leads us into a radical life-change. You're not getting by with anything.

ROMANS 2:1-5, *The Message*, EMPHASIS ADDED

That message is sobering. God is love but His love is not blind. Our deeds, our thoughts, and our very hearts convict us. But the good news comes later in Paul's missive. There is no condemnation in Christ Jesus.[10] He is our hope.

Author Russell Moore proposes a helpful strategy.

For too long, we've called unbelievers to "invite Jesus into your life." Jesus doesn't want to be in your life. Your life's a wreck. Jesus calls you into his life. And his life isn't boring or purposeless or static. It's wild and exhilarating and unpredictable.[11]

My life is a wreck. The lives of the people I am carelessly judging are a wreck. As I prepared to go out to the Oakland A's ballpark, I thought about how our little community of

Jesus followers does not understand a key principle that winning baseball teams know well.

A great team celebrates the strengths of each player and works together to offset the weaknesses. New York Yankees second baseman Joe Gordon immediately comes to mind. Here are a few stats from his 1942 season. He struck out more than any batter in the American League, made more errors that year than any other player in his position, and hit into more double plays than anyone else. You would think that stellar performance would make the ball club start looking for a new second baseman. But there was one mitigating factor.

Gordon won the American League Most Valuable Player for that season.

In spite of his flaws Joe Gordon had a great season. He batted .322, fourth in the American League, with 18 homers and 103 runs batted in. Gordon teamed with Phil Rizzuto to lead the league in double plays turned defensively. Despite some obvious weaknesses in his game, Joe Gordon deserved the MVP honor.

Too often we dwell on the weaknesses and not the talents that God has given others. Or we acknowledge the talents but make a bigger deal about the weaknesses. All of us are a mix of gifts and flaws. Henri Nouwen said, "To the degree that we embrace the truth that our identity is not rooted in our success, power, or popularity, but in God's infinite love, to that degree can we let go of our need to judge."[12]

I need to let go of my need to judge. My identity is not found in feeling superior to someone else, as enticing as that can be. My real identity is found in the amazing redemptive grace of Jesus who calls me His friend. That is consistent and real. I pray that the Holy Spirit will break my heart for all the things that break Jesus' heart and that I will see through His eyes.

I appreciate the lesson, Maggie. As I give grace to my rescued puppy who carries unknown baggage, I am learning to give grace to people, too. Joni and I are seeing progress with Maggie, thanks to patient love and affirmation. She trusts us more each day and accepts our affection. She is relaxing and settling into her forever home.

Her example compels me to express my own gratefulness. "Thank You, Father, for loving and accepting me despite my baggage, and for surrounding me with people who do the same." I am getting better at trusting and accepting that affection as I look forward with confidence to my forever home.

CHAPTER 18

SIT! STAY!

Dogs act exactly the way we would act if we had no shame.

~CYNTHIA HEIMEL

Journal Entry

Maggie is a Labrador puppy mixed with some other mystery DNA. She is a bouncing, wiggling, sixty-pound bundle of unrestrained energy. Whenever she sees a new person, she cannot stop herself from jumping. Oddly enough, some people do not enjoy sixty-pound creatures hurdling pell-mell into their personal space. Weird. So we either need to fix this bad behavior or become hermits.

Today we enrolled Maggie in puppy training classes. One of the first things the instructor, Tony, said was both apparent and profound.

"First of all, you have to teach her to sit and stay. When she is sitting, she can't jump and misbehave."

Thank you, Captain Obvious. Wait a minute. Is this another lesson for me in my discipleship-by-dog journey? Maggie needed to learn to sit to avoid committing doggie offenses. I need to sit, too, in a spiritual sense. The truth is, when I *abide* (the biblical version of "sitting") in Christ, I am empowered to resist sin.

But how can I abide? What does that even mean?

The first time I heard the word *abide* used was in a lesson taken from the Gospel of John in the King James Version, the Bible I read growing up.

> Abide in me, and I in you. As the branch cannot bear fruit of itself, except it abide in the vine; no more can ye, except ye abide in me. I am the vine, ye are the branches: He that abideth in me, and I in him, the same bringeth forth much fruit: for without me ye can do nothing.
>
> JOHN 15:4-5, KJV

I knoweth not about thee, but verily I was confused. When I looked up the definition of *abide* later, it helped clarify what it meant. Abide: (1) to accept something or someone unpleasant; (2) living somewhere; (3) to remain or continue. That was it—to remain or continue—or in Maggie's terms, "to stay." Other Bible translations have captured that nuance of abiding or "staying" in Jesus.

> Remain in me, and I will remain in you. For a branch cannot produce fruit if it is severed from the vine, and you cannot be fruitful unless you remain in me. Yes, I

am the vine; you are the branches. Those who remain in me, and I in them, will produce much fruit. For apart from me you can do nothing.

JOHN 15:4-5

Jesus' message to His followers is to simply remain constantly aware of who we are and where our strength and dependence must be found. It's tempting and easy to make it all about us instead of Jesus; Satan will always seek to engage us in bad and/or good things *if* either one takes our eyes off Jesus. If I am wholly absorbed in spiritual things apart from Christ, things I do more to impress others and hope those wonderful deeds will ensure my salvation, I am engaging in good, but not life-changing endeavors.

We are branches that need to be connected to the Vine. We are not to be independent vines but dependent branches of the life-giving Vine.

I think that we misunderstand the phrase "apart from me you can do nothing." Of course I can do something and often even significant things apart from Jesus. I can have success, make money, and maybe achieve fame. But there is one significant thing that we absolutely cannot do apart from Christ: produce fruit that pleases God. The branch cannot produce fruit when it is disconnected from the vine.

Jesus is the true Vine, and if I am joined to Him I will produce fruit. He doesn't say I *might* produce fruit. He doesn't say I *could* produce fruit if the circumstances are right. Or that I will *occasionally* bear fruit. Jesus says that if I remain in Him I *will* produce much fruit. If I don't remain in Him, I become barren and worthless to Him and His Kingdom.

How do we produce the fruit that Jesus is describing? By not allowing our relationship with Christ to be broken, for us—the branches—not to be severed from the Vine. Our connection to Jesus is not a one-time or yearly or monthly or weekly or daily synchronization. It is not like the intermittent syncs I perform between my computer and phone to update information. It is a continual awareness of our connection to Christ. That connection allows the fruit of the Spirit to grow abundantly in us and become a part of who we are. The apostle Paul describes exactly what kind of fruit that is.

> The Holy Spirit produces this kind of fruit in our lives: love, joy, peace, patience, kindness, goodness, faithfulness, gentleness, and self-control.
>
> GALATIANS 5:22-23

By remaining in an unbroken connection with Christ, we begin to take on His character and produce that kind of fruit. But it can only happen if we "stay" constantly in that relationship.

It didn't take long for Maggie's dog trainer to pinpoint another clue to her behavior. "Maggie is not being belligerent. She has learned to fend for herself. Maggie views you as a caretaker and not a leader. She needs to see you as the leader that she can follow."

It made perfect sense. Maggie accepted our gifts of food and a comfortable bed, but in her mind, she was still in charge. Joni and I wrongly assumed that Maggie was being manipulative when all she was really communicating was, "Somebody needs to be in charge, and since you're not stepping up as a leader, I guess it's my job." Over the weeks, when we consistently took on the role of leader and loved her, she willingly submitted.

That lesson has hit a little too close to home for me. I have accepted with varying degrees of gratitude God's gifts of forgiveness, grace, and salvation. But too often I'm guilty of wanting to fend for myself and be the leader. "Thank You, Lord, for everything, but I prefer to be in charge."

The gospel says I need to get over me and get with Him. I need to constantly remind myself of the radical and reckless joyride that the gospel of grace makes possible. Author Dane Ortlund says it well.

It's time to enjoy grace anew—not the decaffeinated grace that pats us on the hand, ignores our deepest rebellions and doesn't change us, but the high-octane grace that takes our conscience by the scruff of the neck and breathes new life into us with a pardon so scandalous that we cannot help but be changed. It's time to blow aside the hazy cloud of condemnation that hangs over us throughout the day with the strong wind of gospel grace. You "are not under law but under grace" (Rom. 6:14). Jesus is real; grace is defiant; life is short; risk is good. For many of us the time has come to abandon once and for all our play-it-safe, toe-dabbling Christianity and dive in. It's time, as [Robert Farrar] Capon put it, to get drunk on grace—200-proof, defiant grace.[1]

In chapter 8, I talked about the importance of shaking off the sin that slows us down and trips us up. Even though it sounds like a daunting and even impossible task, the author of Hebrews sums up how to do that in one powerful sentence: "We do this by keeping our eyes on Jesus, the champion who initiates and perfects our faith" (12:2).

That is it. There is no other way to consistently live that life apart from keeping our eyes on Jesus. It was a principle that the apostle Peter illustrated clearly for us in this familiar story.

> The boat was far out to sea when the wind came up against them and they were battered by the waves. At about four o'clock in the morning, Jesus came toward them walking on the water. They were scared out of their wits. "A ghost!" they said, crying out in terror.
>
> But Jesus was quick to comfort them. "Courage, it's me. Don't be afraid."

I love how the impetuous faith of Peter (and me) is captured in the next verses.

> Peter, suddenly bold, said, "Master, if it's really you, call me to come to you on the water."
>
> He said, "Come ahead."
>
> Jumping out of the boat, Peter walked on the water to Jesus.

It was going great for the "suddenly bold" Peter when he kept his eyes on Jesus and walked in faith. And then . . .

> But when he looked down at the waves churning beneath his feet, he lost his nerve and started to sink. He cried, "Master, save me!"
>
> Jesus didn't hesitate. He reached down and grabbed his hand. Then he said, "Faint-heart, what got into you?"
>
> MATTHEW 14:24-31, *The Message*

The same is true for me. When I keep my eyes on Jesus, I have the strength to be bold and the ability to produce fruit that is pleasing to God. When Maggie cannot settle down, I tell her to sit so she can focus on calming down and doing the right thing. When she stays and regroups, things go well for her. When my thought life and actions cannot settle down, I need the Holy Spirit to firmly but lovingly tell me to sit . . . stay . . . abide.

Only then do I realize that I have turned my eyes away from Jesus. When I stay, I can focus on His peace, love, forgiveness, and grace, and have the ability to resist sin.

If I am anxious, fearful, have doubts, or am sad, I need to sit, stay, and abide, looking at the One who initiates and perfects my faith.

The apostle Paul spent a little over two years teaching and discipling the new believers in Ephesus before he continued on his missionary journey. It didn't take long for the once-zealous converts to revert to their old habits of immorality, lying, stealing, and gossiping. In other words, things were a mess in the Ephesian church. Paul, who had witnessed the believers' initial spiritual fervor, got wind of what had happened and wrote a letter to the church's leaders to address this sad turn of events.

His letter is nothing like the one I would have zipped off to Ephesus if I had been in Paul's sandals. My letter would have started, "What is wrong with you people? Don't you know how embarrassing this is, especially since I sacrificed so much for you?" But Paul doesn't do that; in fact, he *never* mentioned how badly they had botched things until halfway through the letter. Rather, he begins by reminding these errant followers who they are, praying heartfelt words for them.

Ever since I first heard of your strong faith in the Lord
Jesus and your love for God's people everywhere, I
have not stopped thanking God for you. I pray for you
constantly, asking God, the glorious Father of our Lord
Jesus Christ, to give you spiritual wisdom and insight so
that you might grow in your knowledge of God. I pray
that your hearts will be flooded with light so that you
can understand the confident hope he has given to those
he called—his holy people who are his rich and glorious
inheritance.

I also pray that you will understand the incredible
greatness of God's power for us who believe him. This
is the same mighty power that raised Christ from the
dead and seated him in the place of honor at God's right
hand in the heavenly realms.

EPHESIANS 1:15-20

You get through storms and trials by remembering who
you are. Paul wonderfully reminded the Ephesians that they
had been adopted, redeemed, and sealed. And then he prayed
for them again.

When I think of all this, I fall to my knees and pray to
the Father, the Creator of everything in heaven and on
earth. I pray that from his glorious, unlimited resources
he will empower you with inner strength through his
Spirit. Then Christ will make his home in your hearts as
you trust in him. Your roots will grow down into God's
love and keep you strong. And may you have the power
to understand, as all God's people should, how wide,
how long, how high, and how deep his love is. May you
experience the love of Christ, though it is too great to

understand fully. Then you will be made complete with all the fullness of life and power that comes from God.

Now all glory to God, who is able, through his mighty power at work within us, to accomplish infinitely more than we might ask or think. Glory to him in the church and in Christ Jesus through all generations forever and ever! Amen.

EPHESIANS 3:14-21

I would imagine the church leaders opened Paul's letter with fear, trembling, and shame. They expected to be excoriated but they were lavished with grace instead. They had failed, but Paul reminded them of the Person who had not failed. Only after first affirming His love did Paul begin to address their sin.

What a difference between that approach and what too many of us experience. We tend to address the sin first. Stop that! Quit! Do better! And by the way, Jesus loves you. Or worse, He will love you when you do better. Paul took the grace exit instead. Remember who you are! You are saints! Beloved! Adopted! Redeemed! Those same truths are ours to claim as we

Sit.

Stay.

Abide.

Eyes on Jesus.

When we quit fighting to get better and do those four simple things, something amazing happens. We get better.

Following Jesus is far from effortless; it requires work. But I would suggest that our real assignment is to focus on Him and recognize how much that impacts our lives. To get our eyes off ourselves truly is hard work, a sacrifice.

My old self has been crucified with Christ. It is no
longer I who live, but Christ lives in me. *So I live in this
earthly body by trusting in the Son of God*, who loved me
and gave himself for me.

GALATIANS 2:20, EMPHASIS ADDED

When I forget those truths and I am tempted to sin, I
will simply remember what I tell Maggie when she is out of
line. When she is jumping up and playfully lunging at us, I
have to speak truth into her life. She is a big girl who needs
to learn what her boundaries are. She needs to settle down
or a playful moment will turn into a time-out. So I calmly
but firmly speak to her.

Sit.

Stay.

Maggie is learning that she is rewarded when she sits and
stays. She will get to play, have treats, or receive the affection
that she was hoping to receive.

She is teaching this old dog that I need continuous
refresher courses too.

CHAPTER 19

GENTLY LEADING

It seems to me that the good Lord in his infinite wisdom
gave us three things to make life bearable—hope, jokes
and dogs, but the greatest of these was dogs.

~ROBYN DAVIDSON, *TRACKS: ONE WOMAN'S JOURNEY*
ACROSS 1,700 MILES OF AUSTRALIAN OUTBACK

Journal Entry

Today Maggie took me out for a drag. I would prefer that her idea of a walk would more closely resemble mine, so we have some work to do. I either need to find a way to train her not to pull me around the neighborhood or rescue ten more Labs just like her and enter the Iditarod dogsled race. I don't particularly care for freezing to death, so I think I will work on training Maggie to walk instead of pull.

Maggie has definitely made progress learning her commands, but I knew that she needed some extra help on the walking front. A tip from our trainer led us to a device called the Gentle Leader. He demonstrated how it works and we were sold. It's a harness that fits over the dog's head and snout but it isn't as restrictive as a muzzle can be; Maggie is free to sniff, drink, and explore without restriction. After getting fitted at the store, we went home and gave our new device a try. It was, in a word, amazing.

Maggie made a couple of attempts to take control, but with a small tug I let her know that I was the leader and she complied without a struggle. I had learned that many dogs instinctively pull on a traditional leash or shoulder harness. Maggie had great instincts on that front. With the new harness I can easily and gently redirect her. It was like someone snuck in the house and swapped a new dog for Maggie. (For everyone's information, I'm not a paid spokesperson for Gentle Leader—just a satisfied dog owner.)

I reflected on the remarkable difference later that day. Before I found this solution, Maggie fought for control, a force I struggled to contain. With the Gentle Leader she quickly submitted to me as the leader of our little pack. She was more relaxed, happier, and a lot more fun to be with on our daily journey.

Of course, there was a lesson in this for me, too. God's sense of timing of these little lessons can be amusing or irritating to me. This time it was irritating. I had been in a period of fighting for control in my own journey with Jesus. Sure, I wanted to walk with Him. Yet in my heart I reserved the right to pull, divert, and take control when I felt insecure that God was really in control and questioning if He understood what I was going through. That admission looks worse in print than it sounded in my mind.

Jesus talks about how we limit our ability to have peace when we don't allow Him to provide us with strength. He didn't mention a harness, but a yoke, and that His yoke is "easy."

Jesus said, "Come to me, all of you who are weary and
carry heavy burdens, and I will give you rest. Take my
yoke upon you. Let me teach you, because I am humble
and gentle at heart, and you will find rest for your souls.
For my yoke is easy to bear, and the burden I give you is
light."

MATTHEW 11:28-30

We don't have to ride the roller coaster of life more than
a couple of times to know that this journey is not "easy." I
thought about losses I have suffered in my life and some of
the struggles that I am dealing with today. I was puzzled.
What did Jesus mean by that statement, "My yoke is easy"?
Clearly, the burdens of life are heavy. There is nothing easy
about heartache, pain, and loss.

I reread Jesus' inviting words: "Come to me." No one
needs to go through life's difficulties alone, but the truth is
that Jesus will not force Himself on you. You have permission
to come to Jesus whenever you are ready.

In Jesus' day, oxen were harnessed together with a wooden
yoke, a beam that fit over the animals' shoulders to keep
them moving together in one direction. The oxen shared the
effort to accomplish the task. That idea fit quite well into my
performance-driven faith. Of course Jesus is with me, but I
decided that I had to pull my weight. The only problem with
my view was that it was unbiblical and even dangerous.

In this passage Jesus is not speaking of physical burdens.
The truth is that Jesus was talking about the yoke of the
Torah, the yoke of the law of Moses, which his Jewish listen-
ers would have known well. The Old Testament yoke represented submission to authority. The Jews knew that the law
was impossible to keep, but they kept trying. Jesus was offering

them His yoke of grace. Compared to the impossible standards of the Pharisees and the law, His way was easy. Agreed.

Jesus makes another important offer. "*Let me teach you,* because I am humble and gentle at heart."

For years, I strained to pull my weight by dogged (pardon the pun) effort, while Jesus quietly offered a better way. I don't have to figure this out to be loved by Jesus. I just need to be available.

"Let me teach you."

I wore myself out trying to do more to please Him, even as He whispered, "I am humble and gentle at heart. Your trust and faith please Me, not your joyless self-efforts to be better."

Members of that agrarian culture of Jesus' time would have known that you train a young ox by pairing it with an experienced ox. The mature ox would carry the bulk of the burden as the younger one walked by its side and learned. Author Jim Botts relayed the strategy of a wise farmer.

> Well you see, it's like this. That older ox is the best
> ox that I have ever had; he knows his way around the
> field. The reason I put the younger one with him is
> so the older, more knowledgeable ox could teach him
> how to plow. If I never put them together the younger
> one would never learn. By himself the younger ox
> would pull himself to death, but together he learns to
> cooperate with and rest in the strength of the older ox.[1]

That is a beautiful image. Jesus walking alongside me, but carrying the burden as I learn from Him. I don't need to strain myself in an attempt to shoulder everything on my own; Jesus wants me to be willing to gently submit to His strength and not rely solely on mine. He is extending an offer to those who are exhausted, emotionally drained, and buckling under what life brings. Pain and loss are a given in this life, but it is comforting to know that I can find rest for my weary soul, even as I grieve and doubt and waver. When I am exhausted, I can take time and seek respite in Him.

Too many faith communities have gotten this wrong. Pastor Tullian Tchividjian summarizes the struggle powerfully. "Jesus didn't say, 'Come to me all who are weary and I will give you a to-do list to keep me loving you.' He said 'I will give you rest.'"[2] Jesus never intended for us to carry around long to-do lists. As we struggle mightily to try to earn what we already have, He must look upon us sorrowfully, knowing how much He can help.

"My yoke is easy." Yokes were custom fitted to each individual ox. If the fit was incorrect, the yoke would rub and hurt the ox, making the animal reluctant to keep going. If the yoke was perfectly fitted, it was easy for the ox to endure. A master carpenter would find the right ratio of strength and weight, whittling the yoke down to do its job, which meant the ox was able to work longer without tiring. The same is true for all of you, Jesus says. I will "fit" each one of you perfectly with the yoke that you can bear and no more.

Justin Martyr, whose life was transformed when he became a follower of Christ, was an ardent defender of the Christian faith. He wrote in the mid-second century (only about eighty years after the book of Mark, the first written Gospel) that Jesus was a carpenter who built yokes and plows like his father before him.[3] Justin noted that Jesus used His knowledge of carpentry to teach the symbols of righteousness to His followers. Oral tradition says that Jesus made such perfectly fitting yokes that people came from miles around to have their oxen measured and fitted by Him. Whether that was true or not, the fact remains that Jesus certainly understood what a yoke was and how effective it was, both practically and spiritually.

When I finally stopped trying to do all the work in order to feel accepted by Christ, no longer restrained by the harness of legalism and relaxed in the "gentle leading" of grace, I was free to be fully alive in Christ.

Jesus wants you to don His yoke. Trust Him. Have faith. He has done the heavy lifting already. Rest in Him. Learn how to be humble and gentle in spirit. Quit trying so dadgum (that may not be in the Greek) hard and serve out of grateful love. Jesus tells us when we believe those truths, our burdens are light. The walk with Him is easy and natural.

I think of that as I watch Maggie romp excitedly around the house after seeing me get my walking shoes and headset. She is eager and joyful on our morning walks now that she knows I am going to lead.

She can relax and take in everything around her because she realizes that she doesn't need to be in control. Point taken.

CHAPTER 20

LIFE INTERRUPTED

Dogs are on vacation every time they go out the door.

~ANONYMOUS

Journal Entry

Today Maggie and I traversed the usual path. She sniffed and I listened to a podcast as we paced briskly through a comfortable Texas fall morning. She spotted something and moved toward the curb. My eye caught something at the same time, and I jerked violently on her leash to pull her toward me.

She looked surprised, puzzled at what she had done wrong for such a harsh correction from me. The truth was that she hadn't done anything wrong. Some knucklehead had shattered a beer bottle and a jagged piece was right in her path. She could have been seriously cut by the razor-sharp glass. I was thankful I

had spotted it, but I could see that my action confused
and maybe hurt Maggie's feelings. I needed to assure
her that my unexpected reaction was not punitive but
entirely out of my love and concern for her.

I immediately dropped down to my knee, scratched Maggie's ears, and verbally praised her. "It's okay, girl. Everything's okay. It's okay."

I was glad that she perked up immediately. Her uncertainty vanished, her drooping tail began to wag, and her beautiful eyes brightened again. She understood we were good again. It was another lesson for me to ponder.

How many times have I responded in confusion and hurt when God gently or not so gently pulled me off a path of destruction when I had no idea what He was doing? Oh, that I would trust and love God as much as Maggie trusts and loves me. Instead I start second-guessing when God throws me a curve or allows a high-and-tight fastball to knock me on my keister. I get out the transgression magnifying glass to detect which sin might have caused God to withdraw His favor from me, occasionally throwing pleading glances heavenward.

Right on cue during the morning walk, Pastor Tullian Tchividjian answered my question with this insight.

Until we see God-sent storms as interventions and not punishments, we'll never get better, we'll only get bitter. Some difficult circumstances you're facing right now may well be a God-sent storm of mercy intended to be his intervention in your life. You're in danger, and either you don't realize it or you're living in denial.[1]

Precisely. God sees the jagged glass that I am about to step on and He pulls me back in love. The problem isn't with Him; it's my response to the correction. I am shocked and hurt, then I pout—the Dave Burchett default mode. *Thanks, Maggie, I need to pay attention to your lesson. You were startled and hurt when I gave you such a strong correction, but then you instinctively looked at me.* As soon as I assured her that I loved her and all was okay, she was fine. Simple for her, and it should be for me, too. I am still learning to trust that God loves me when I feel He is disciplining me.

I think we have a hard time distinguishing between punishment and discipline. Paul Tautges dispenses this biblical counsel.

> Punishment casts away, while discipline restores.
> Punishment is for subjects of wrath, while discipline
> is for children of God. Punishment requires payment
> for sin, while discipline corrects to protect and
> bless, because sin has already been paid for by Jesus.
> Punishment focuses on past sins, whereas discipline,
> while still dealing with sin, looks to the future
> blessing of obedience that follows true repentance.
> This is why punishment often provokes believers
> to wrath while biblical discipline works to produce
> sorrow leading to repentance.[2]

In the New Living Translation the passage heading for the first twelve verses in Hebrews 12 is spot on: "God's Discipline Proves His Love."[3]

For too many years I thought God's corrective actions were punishment that proved His displeasure, when in actuality that discipline proved His love.

Have you forgotten the encouraging words God spoke
to you as his children? He said,

"My child, don't make light of the LORD's discipline,
    and don't give up when he corrects you.
For the LORD disciplines those he loves,
    and he punishes each one he accepts as his child."

As you endure this divine discipline, remember that
God is treating you as his own children. Who ever heard
of a child who is never disciplined by its father? If God
doesn't discipline you as he does all of his children, it
means that you are illegitimate and are not really his
children at all. Since we respected our earthly fathers
who disciplined us, shouldn't we submit even more
to the discipline of the Father of our spirits, and live
forever?

For our earthly fathers disciplined us for a few
years, doing the best they knew how. But God's
discipline is always good for us, so that we might share
in his holiness. No discipline is enjoyable while it is
happening—it's painful! But afterward there will be
a peaceful harvest of right living for those who are
trained in this way.

HEBREWS 12:5-11

Even as a self-confessed imperfect father (corroborating
evidence available from all three sons), I distinctly remember that I disciplined my children so they would grow up
to be honest, kind, and loving. I didn't want to make their
lives miserable, stick it to them, or make them sad. On the
contrary, I wanted them to learn how to live joyfully and

well. If a flawed earthly father can have that heartfelt desire, how much more does my heavenly Father desire my growth and good? It is all in understanding the motive behind the action.

Punishment is focused on a past mistake. Punishment may be deserved and it may prevent future mistakes and bad decisions, but it cannot result in redemption. Punishment produces negative emotions like shame, fear, guilt, regret, and helplessness. Discipline has an entirely different result.

Discipline is focused on future growth and is all about redemption. The purpose of punishment is to impose pain for wrongdoing. Discipline desires to correct us so that we will mature in our faith.

What does it mean that God administers His discipline in the realm of grace? It means that all His teaching, training, and discipline are administered in love and for our spiritual welfare. It means that God is never angry with us, though He is often grieved at our sins. It means He does not condemn us or count our sins against us. All that He does in us and to us is done on the basis of unmerited favor.[4]

I know there were moments when I punished my boys. I wanted them to pay for their behavior. I regret those moments and hope they were rare. But I also know that there were moments when my heart was flooded with love and compassion and I only desired to correct them for their benefit. I knew they were making choices that were not the best. I wanted to be able to lovingly direct them so they would grow in character. Those moments of deep desire to love my boys even if it was painful for our relationship are just a fraction of the infinite desire that God has for me to mature for His glory.

It's okay to be surprised and even sad when we are disciplined. But I'm taking Maggie's response to heart. When she looked at her master and saw that she was still loved, Maggie relaxed, turned, and kept on walking. The journey continues for both of us.

CHAPTER 21

THE HIDDEN TOXICITY OF FORBIDDEN FRUIT

If you live with dogs, you'll never run out of things to write about.

~SHARON DELAROSE

JOURNAL ENTRY

A lovely day with Joni ended in a not-so-lovely fashion tonight at an emergency pet clinic. After buying a large container of red grapes at Costco, we rinsed them off in our deep sink, left them to dry, and went out to run a couple more errands. We never dreamed that Maggie would be able to reach anything in that deep sink. However, she dreamed that she could and her dream came true. We returned to find a delighted Labrador sitting among scattered grape stems. She had consumed about two pounds of grapes. A quick online search revealed that even a few grapes could be toxic . . . let alone a couple of pounds. So we were

*off to the emergency clinic to empty her stomach and
my wallet.*

Fortunately, Joni and I returned home before the forbidden fruit Maggie had swallowed had a chance to digest. We
got her to the vet in time to induce several rounds of vomit-
ing that kept the potentially deadly toxins from getting into
her digestive tract. You don't think of grapes as being harm-
ful, especially when grapes are part of many animals' regular
diet. But we learned that grapes are a no-no for dogs and cats,
because they can cause kidney failure and organ shutdown.

After we had been there awhile, a veterinary assistant
called me into a back room to survey Maggie's "work" to
determine if she had expelled all the grapes that I suspected
she might have eaten. She was sprawled on the floor with
paws splayed out, looking like a seasick sailor on rough seas.
I couldn't help but be impressed with how many disgusting
remains of grape skins and stems were there. But I wasn't sure
if that represented her entire raid so the clinic staff induced
one more round to be safe.

The good news is that Maggie was fine after she spent
an uncomfortable evening of purging her counter-surfing
sin. She walked unsteadily to the car and came home to
sleep it off.

The lesson was striking. Maggie knows she is not supposed to get food off the counter. She also knew that her
master was gone, so the temptation was overwhelming. In
her doggie brain the gratification of those delicious grapes
offset the potential risk of getting caught. I am not sure if
dogs can rationalize, but if they could, Maggie would have
pointed out that she left half the grapes for us.

It wasn't getting in trouble with me that posed the biggest

risk for her. The scary thing was that the forbidden fruit could have killed her. The immediate gratification of a tasty snack could have destroyed her kidneys and ended her very young life. Maggie had no clue what danger she had put herself in.

When I left the slightly green and unsteady Maggie after another round of purging, I said to the attending vet, "Maybe this will teach her the next time."

"Nope," she replied with a smile. "She lives in the moment."

I know. Same song. Second verse—this time from a different vet with a less-than-positive twist. For dogs and people, forbidden fruit is attractive. It often is sweet. It is tantalizing. But if we don't see the danger, it can be poisonous. Maggie's foray into forbidden fruit ended with a scare and a memorable story. For too many others, forbidden fruit can destroy a marriage, a family, the body, and the soul.

On the way home I thought about what the vet said. *I hope that Maggie has more sense than to go right back to the grapes that she just tossed up unceremoniously.* And then I considered a very uncomfortable truth. We supposedly brainier creatures do exactly the same thing.

We are repulsed after visiting an Internet porn site and then return hours later. We wake up feeling terrible after a night of partying and repeat the cycle within twenty-four hours. We feel guilty about an inappropriate relationship as we plan the next rendezvous. We regret gossiping about a colleague until it's our chance to dish up a juicy tidbit. We vow to be kind until stress and tiredness overwhelm our restraint and we lose it.

We continually go back and do what we tell ourselves we will never do again. I spent decades in a frustrating spiritual version of the inane shampoo instructions, "Lather. Rinse. Repeat."

Sin. Repent. Repeat.

Albert Einstein has been credited as saying that "insanity is doing the same thing over and over again and expecting different results." I am not quite willing to concede that I was insane, but the truth is that for years I did approach my spiritual life the same way every day while somehow expecting different results.

I would make a *mistake* (politically correct for *sin*), and I would convince myself that I would never do that again. I was grateful that the consequences were not worse. I was determined to stay far, far away from that sin. And then before I knew it, I had forgotten the promise to do better and repeated the sin. The apostle Paul wrote about this very thing in his letter to the Romans.

> I decide to do good, but I don't *really* do it; I decide not to do bad, but then I do it anyway. My decisions, such as they are, don't result in actions. Something has gone wrong deep within me and gets the better of me every time.
> ROMANS 7:19-20, *The Message*

Wow . . . can I relate to that. A few sentences later, Paul admits,

> I've tried everything and nothing helps. I'm at the end of my rope. Is there no one who can do anything for me? Isn't that the real question?
> ROMANS 7:24, *The Message*

That *is* the real question. And there is a real answer offered by Paul.

The answer, thank God, is that Jesus Christ can and does. He acted to set things right in this life of contradictions where I want to serve God with all my heart and mind, but am pulled by the influence of sin to do something totally different.

ROMANS 7:25, *The Message*

So what can you do to get out of this sin spiral?

Nothing.

Wait! Don't get depressed. This is good news. You and I can't do it. I am incapable of escaping my spiritual treadmill through my own efforts. Only Jesus can enable me to escape this endless loop of frustration. Paul reveals what needs to happen.

If God himself has taken up residence in your life, you can hardly be thinking more of yourself than of him.

ROMANS 8:9, *The Message*

Allow the truth of that verse to soak in. That is the key. The way to sin less is to think less about sin and more about Jesus. Focusing on sin increases sin. Focusing on Jesus denies sin's power.

Want to get out of your sin-repent-repeat existence? Most of us who wanted to do that realized we couldn't deal with our sin separation from God on our own. We needed Jesus. So why do we think we can deal with our ongoing sin issues on our own? When the Father looks at me on my very worst day, this is who He sees:

Jesus.

That is Step 1. I don't have to clean up the sin to please God. He loves me already because of Jesus.

Step 2. I need to recognize daily that the Spirit of God has taken up residence in my life.

I am learning that I am the one who limits His power by restricting access and control to my thoughts and actions. I am learning that I don't need to live with the frustrating effects of repeated self-effort. Instead, I can trust God, trust that Jesus has my sin covered, and trust that the Spirit of God will allow me to resolve that sin. When I trust God and what His Word says to be true, it allows me to escape the maddening pattern of sin-repent-repeat. Instead I have a new life full of possibilities to thank God for His amazing grace.

Maggie never realized the potential toxicity of her forbidden fruit. She was blissful in her ignorance. While I may imitate that tactic, I can't use that as an excuse. God's Word and the gentle conviction of the Holy Spirit warn His followers that forbidden fruit will harm us.

Maggie made a choice and got sick. The choice I make can have far more devastating and even eternal consequences. Spiritual forbidden fruit can have unseen and deadly toxins for my relationship to God, family, and friends. God gives us so much freedom to find joy within the structure of family, marriage, community, work, and worship. Yet we still think that there is one thing that God might be withholding from us that will bring us happiness. That idea was wrong for Adam and Eve in the Garden of Eden and continues to be wrong today. God has given us everything we need to be content and joyful.

David wrote that the real source of joy is not more success or more stuff.

> Why is everyone hungry for *more*? "More, more," they say.

"More, more."
I have God's more-than-enough,
More joy in one ordinary day

Than they get in all their shopping sprees.
At day's end I'm ready for sound sleep,
For you, GOD, have put my life back together.

PSALM 4:6-8, *The Message*

A quick and expensive visit to the doggie ER helped Maggie recover from her ill-advised food adventure. The reminder for me is that forbidden fruit never delivers on its promise. I begin with God's "more-than-enough" every day, and I am grateful for that. May I never take that gift for granted.

CHAPTER 22

O MAGGIE, WHERE ART THOU?

Dogs are great. Bad dogs, if we can really call them
that, are perhaps the greatest of them all.

~JOHN GROGAN, *MARLEY & ME: LIFE AND LOVE*
WITH THE WORLD'S WORST DOG

Journal Entry

It is usually not a good thing when my wife calls and leads with this question: "Guess what your dog did today?" One of those calls relayed how Maggie jumped through a window screen in pursuit of a bug.

This morning I got another call and heard that dreaded possessive pronoun again. However, there was a light tone to Joni's voice that promised a good story. Joni was leaving for church and Maggie was missing in action. She called Maggie. Nothing. After a few minutes' investigation, Joni uncovered the reason for Maggie's vanishing act. She had decided to revisit a bad behavior that she had abandoned

*for several weeks. Joni found two freshly dug holes in
the backyard. As my wife checked out the damage,
she looked around for Maggie and spotted something
across the yard.*

*It was Maggie, hiding behind a tree and peeking
around every few seconds to see if the coast was
clear. Joni started laughing and ran for the camera.
Apparently, it is hard for a long-legged, seventy-pound
Lab to hide completely behind a skinny tree. But
Maggie thought if she could stay hidden for a while
everything would be okay.*

In my mind's eye I could just picture Maggie's attempt,
and I was glad it was captured for posterity. It was ridiculous
for Maggie to try to hide when she was caught red-pawed,
er, red-handed. The idea that she could cover up her bad
behavior by hiding seemed pretty silly.

Ah, another lesson. What is always my first impulse when
I sin? To hide. I especially want to hide my failure from Joni
if she would be impacted by it. I want to hide my disappoint-
ing behavior from my friends. And, astonishingly, I guess I
think I can hide my sin from God. I must look as ridiculous
to Jesus when I try to hide from Him as Maggie's big old
dog feet and long snout peeking around that too-small tree
appeared to Joni.

At least my response is not a unique behavior. It has been
true of all humanity, from the moment it happened in the
Garden of Eden.

Now the serpent was more shrewd than any of the wild
animals that the LORD God had made. He said to the
woman, "Is it really true that God said, 'You must not

eat from any tree of the orchard'?" The woman said to the serpent, "We may eat of the fruit from the trees of the orchard; but concerning the fruit of the tree that is in the middle of the orchard God said, 'You must not eat from it, and you must not touch it, or else you will die.'" The serpent said to the woman, "Surely you will not die, for God knows that when you eat from it your eyes will open and you will be like divine beings who know good and evil."

When the woman saw that the tree produced fruit that was good for food, was attractive to the eye, and was desirable for making one wise, she took some of its fruit and ate it. She also gave some of it to her husband who was with her, and he ate it. Then the eyes of both of them opened, and they knew they were naked; so they sewed fig leaves together and made coverings for themselves.

Then the man and his wife heard the sound of the Lord God moving about in the orchard at the breezy time of the day, and they hid from the Lord God among the trees of the orchard. But the Lord God called to the man and said to him, "Where are you?" The man replied, "I heard you moving about in the orchard, and I was afraid because I was naked, so I hid." And the Lord God said, "Who told you that you were naked? Did you eat from the tree that I commanded you not to eat from?" The man said, "The woman whom you gave me, she gave me some fruit from the tree and I ate it." So the Lord God said to the woman, "What is this you have done?" And the woman replied, "The serpent tricked me, and I ate."

GENESIS 3:1-13, NET

Pastor Tim Keller observed that "in the Garden of Eden, the first lie of the serpent was to make humans disbelieve that God had their best interests in mind."[1] It is a battle that honest followers of Jesus fight to this day. When you feel out of control or things are going badly, you wonder if God really has your best interest on the front burner of His long-term planning. From that lie comes a spectacular smorgasbord of sin.

Look at the behaviors that began on that fateful day and that we continue millennia later. After believing the lie, Adam and Eve realized their sin. Sin revealed their nakedness and vulnerability. The first reaction was to cover up the truth of what they had done. From Creation to today's headlines, we know that a cover-up does not work and usually makes a sin exponentially worse. But we still try.

The second part of the plan was to hide. The problem with hiding is that you're always looking over your shoulder (or around a tree). When Adam was caught, he didn't deny his transgression, he just blamed that woman God had given him. Adam forgot to mention that he apparently stood by and observed all this happening without mustering up the courage to speak up and intervene. Eve admits her actions, too, while blaming the serpent. So in one moment of tragic sin, the human race learned how to covet, misrepresent, rationalize, hide, cover up, blame others, and lie, among other things. That was a very, very bad day.

Sadly, in my own journey of faith I have practiced most if not all of the sins committed (with apologies to Ricky Nelson) at the original Garden party. I have blamed others for my own shortcomings. I have tried to cover up my sins in order to dodge the consequences. For me, the most pernicious tendency I fight is the same one that Maggie tried. I go and hide.

Why do I do that? I think I have to circle back around to Tim Keller's observation that I don't always believe God has my best interest at heart. Unfortunately, that is a pretty easy conclusion when your early teaching centered on a harsh God who was equally willing to send sinners and even badly behaving churchgoers to hell.

Maggie headed behind the tree even though Joni didn't discipline her or get angry. Maggie just thought she had done something wrong, so she decided she needed to hide. I do the same thing. I hide even as God (and others) extends grace and forgiveness to me. I slip on the mask again because I still fear that I will not be loved if they see who I really am.

The satirical publication *The Onion* had a humorous but all-too-close-to-the-truth story recently with the headline, "Report: Today [*sic*] the Day They Find Out You're a Fraud." (Caution: *The Onion* is not always a G-rated site.) The fabricated "research" in the story revealed what I have always feared.

> While experts agree you've been remarkably successful so far at keeping up the ruse that you're a capable, worthwhile individual, a new report out this week indicates that today is the day they finally figure out you're a complete and utter fraud.
>
> The report, compiled by the Pew Research Center, states that sometime within the next 24 hours, people will find out that you have no idea what you're doing, that you've been faking it for years, and that, through continuous lying and shameless posturing, you've actually managed to dupe virtually everyone around you into thinking you're something other than a weak and ineffectual person.[2]

Isn't that how many of us feel? Especially those who are honest about their walk with the Lord? I know how desperately short I fall in my desire to live a life that resembles Christ. So I hide from God and others. There is one major flaw in my instincts. I can hide from you for a while, maybe even forever. But I can't hide from God for even a millisecond. So why do I try?

Adam's first response gives us a clue. "I was afraid because I was naked, so I hid." For a proud and insecure dude like me, that is the answer. Failure makes me feel naked and vulnerable. That makes me afraid. And the next thing I know I am trying to push a seventy-pound Labrador out of the way for a spot behind a tree. I am afraid of looking stupid. Afraid of conflict. Afraid of letting others and God down.

The word *afraid* appears about sixty times in the New Testament. A couple of those passages give me some insight into why I instinctively become afraid and want to hide.

In the first chapters of the Gospel of Mark, we read how Jesus' disciples were eyewitnesses to Jesus' miraculous healings and His power to cast out demons. You would think that would make them pretty confident about what He could do. Fast-forward just a few hours as Mark picks up the story.

As evening came, Jesus said to his disciples, "Let's cross to the other side of the lake." So they took Jesus in the boat and started out, leaving the crowds behind (although other boats followed). But soon a fierce storm came up. High waves were breaking into the boat, and it began to fill with water.

Jesus was sleeping at the back of the boat with his head on a cushion. The disciples woke him up, shouting, "Teacher, don't you care that we're going to drown?"

When Jesus woke up, he rebuked the wind and said to the waves, "Silence! Be still!" Suddenly the wind stopped, and there was a great calm. Then he asked them, "Why are you afraid? Do you still have no faith?"

MARK 4:35-40

Ouch. Why am I afraid? I am "afraid" one answer is that I don't have enough faith. The second reason is found in something that John, Jesus' beloved disciple, wrote in his first letter.

As we live in God, our love grows more perfect. So we will not be afraid on the day of judgment, but we can face him with confidence because we live like Jesus here in this world.

Such love has no fear, because perfect love expels all fear. If we are afraid, it is for fear of punishment, and this shows that we have not fully experienced his perfect love. We love each other because he loved us first.

I JOHN 4:17-19

I am fearful because I do not fully trust His perfect love for me. God is for me and not against me. I am forgiven. God loved me first with a radical and unmerited love. And I don't have to grab some fig leaves to cover my shame and nakedness. I have a cloak of righteousness that covers my shame and sin. I look a whole lot better in the robe of righteousness than I would in fig leaves. Trust me on that one.

It's apparent that Maggie is trusting Joni and me more and more. She is figuring out that we are not going to harm her when she does something wrong—she's hiding less. Whatever had happened in her past that caused her to be fearful is healing. Interestingly enough, as her fear is disappearing, her bad behaviors are diminishing. Hmm . . . sounds like living in grace to me.

So the lesson for Maggie and for me is the same. It is time for both of us to come out of hiding. We are both forgiven.

CHAPTER 23

LEARNING TO LIVE

Dogs come into our lives to teach us about love and loyalty. They depart to teach us about loss. . . . A new dog never replaces an old dog; it merely expands the heart. If you have loved many dogs, your heart is very big.

~ERICA JONG, "A WOMAN'S BEST FRIEND"

WHEN I STARTED THIS JOURNEY of writing about my friend Hannah, I suspected it would only be to prepare my heart for my impending loss. But as the weeks went by, I realized that I could learn a lot about living from my faithful friend. More than anything, she taught me that "preparing for death is preparing for life," a principle that has radically changed my perspective. The corollary truth is when you are not afraid to die you are not afraid to live.

I know that I probably missed some earlier lessons from Hannah because I wasn't thinking of her as my mentor. Still, what I did take in during that unexpected gift of time after her diagnosis provides a blueprint for all of us to live fully and joyfully. Hannah modeled a canine code of conduct that is worth emulating, and I believe Maggie will continue to follow her lead. Here are some of the messages I believe Hannah (and Maggie) wants me to remind you of.

Live in the Moment

Dog trainer Cesar Millan counts on one constant for getting quick results from seemingly "untrainable" dogs. He creates a new environment and behaviors more easily because of this familiar refrain: "Dogs live in the moment. They don't regret the past or worry about the future."[1]

There is no doubt we have a theme here. So simple and yet so profoundly important. When we live in regret of the past or fear of the future, we forfeit the potential joy of today. The psalmist encouraged us to embrace that very idea.

> This is the day the LORD has made. We will rejoice and be glad in it.
> PSALM 118:24

Communicate through Actions, *Then* Words

Maggie responds more to body language and energy than words. If I am calm, she is calm. If I am playful, she is playful. She will respond to my voice commands, but it is really my actions that trigger her immediate, instinctual response.

People who are skeptical about this Christian faith we desire to live before them put more credence in our actions than our words. They need to see it to believe it. Make sure that your actions reflect the fruit of the Spirit; God will ensure that your supply is never depleted. Always err on the side of grace.

> The Holy Spirit produces this kind of fruit in our lives: love, joy, peace, patience, kindness, goodness,

faithfulness, gentleness, and self-control. There is no law against these things!

GALATIANS 5:22-23

Be consistent and full of grace in your communication. God has been teaching me a lot in this area. I am trying to always communicate with both grace and truth. I love that Jesus is described by the apostle John as being full of grace and truth. I suspect in God's wisdom grace comes first because we have a far harder time communicating with grace. I am usually willing to be "honest" and tell you where you are wrong. Doing that with grace and truth requires me to love you and to be vulnerable. It is much easier just to whack you with the rolled-up newspaper of judgment. I am glad Maggie cannot read because she would not approve of that metaphor.

Be wise in the way you act toward outsiders; make the most of every opportunity. Let your conversation be always full of grace, seasoned with salt, so that you may know how to answer everyone.

COLOSSIANS 4:5-6, NIV

Don't Hold Grudges

Cesar Millan has spent a lot of time observing dog behavior and learning how well our canine friends sort things out. "There's a remarkable lack of conflict in dog packs. That's because members resolve the situation when disagreements arise, then move on. Imagine what our world would be like if we dealt with our conflicts before they escalated out of control."[2]

Amen. To quote my friend Bart Millard of MercyMe, "I can only imagine."

This may be the biggest difference between dog packs and

church congregation packs. There is an unsettling amount of conflict in our body of believers. And the reason is that the members of our "pack" too often don't resolve a situation. We get angry and hurt and move on without making peace. Unresolved sin is buried alive and it comes back at surprising moments. A follower of Jesus who does not forgive has forgotten how much he or she has been forgiven. So, as we learned from Miss Hannah, shake off your differences and resolve them. She might also remind you that life is too short and too unpredictable to hold grudges.

> Make allowance for each other's faults, and forgive anyone who offends you. Remember, the Lord forgave you, so you must forgive others.
> COLOSSIANS 3:13

Learn to Sit and Stay!

Maggie learned to sit and stay, which has helped her keep bad behaviors in check. She taught me the importance of sitting and staying (abiding) with my eyes on Jesus instead of on the behavior I am trying to stop. When I quit focusing on the sin and shift to the Savior, the sin dissipates. Why did it take me so long to trust that the One who died for my sins is the One who gives me power over them?

> Just as you received Christ Jesus as Lord, continue to live your lives in him.
> COLOSSIANS 2:6, NIV

Live with Purpose

Dogs are bred for a purpose. Some are retrievers. Some are herders. Each has a purpose programmed into its DNA.

Followers of Jesus are no different. We are called to a purpose. Live like you matter. Why? Because you do.

> I am certain that God, who began the good work within you, will continue his work until it is finally finished on the day when Christ Jesus returns.
>
> PHILIPPIANS 1:6

You have a role in God's eternal story. How cool is that?

Love Unconditionally

Hannah exemplified this lesson every day of her life. I have had the opportunity to pass it forward to Maggie, and she is learning to trust and love unconditionally. This message applies to every person in every relationship, but let me point out three important ones that are significant to me. I want to make them a priority and challenge you to consider doing the same.

Love your wife . . .

Most of us married guys repeated something like this on our wedding day.

> I (Guy in Tux) take you (What Were You Thinking, Beautiful Bride) to be my wife, to have and to hold from this day forward, for better or for worse, for richer, for poorer, in sickness and in health, to love and to cherish, from this day forward until death do us part.

How often do you think of those words, let alone act as if you meant them? If you live and love in the moment, you will take those vows seriously. The word *cherish* is a word that we "tough" guys don't use much. *Merriam-Webster* helps us here. *Cherish* means "to hold dear; feel or show affection for; to keep or cultivate with care and affection." I wish I had cherished Joni more consistently over the years, but I am working to change that. If I live fully in the moment, that should be at the forefront of my thoughts.

Love your children . . .
If you live and love in the moment, you will love your children for who God created them to be and not what you hoped they would become to make you look good. Affirm them with love for who they actually are and the gifts God gave them. Every child is gifted in some areas, just not in all of them. Tell your children how special they are. Tell them when you are proud of them. Tell them you love them. Let them be kids and get dirty and break things once in a while. It's okay. They won't be perfect because—news flash—you aren't either.

Love your friends . . .
If you live and love in the moment, you will forget the petty annoyances that irk you and have kept you from talking to that friend. Let your friends know how much they mean to you and how much you love them. Even when they fail to meet your expectations, you need to love them. In fact, those are the times you *especially* love them.

Love Your Life
Is there a better example of this than a canine companion? If only we could live like we were just let off the leash to run in freedom and joyous abandon. Enjoy the day you have. Sure, life can be hard and often seems unfair. For some, life is really hard. But we do have a choice in how we play the

cards dealt to us. If you live fully in the moment, you revel in what you have around you. Right on cue Maggie just walked in the room, saw her toy, leaped through the air, and grabbed it. Now she is having a blast tossing it around. I know that life can be burdensome, but I suspect we pass by a lot of those spontaneous opportunities for joy each day as we worry about something that may not even happen.

> Always be full of joy in the Lord. I say it again—rejoice! Let everyone see that you are considerate in all you do. Remember, the Lord is coming soon.
> Don't worry about anything; instead, pray about everything. Tell God what you need, and thank him for all he has done. Then you will experience God's peace, which exceeds anything we can understand. His peace will guard your hearts and minds as you live in Christ Jesus.
> PHILIPPIANS 4:4-7

Love to Laugh

Maggie laughs with her eyes. Dogs speak through those amazing eyes and their body language. I have read that a dog can express more with her tail in minutes than her owner can with his tongue (or keyboard) in hours. Everyone who knows me at all knows that I love to laugh. I have adopted the philosophy that if an embarrassing moment is going to make you chuckle a year from now, you might as well start laughing today. Learn to laugh at yourself. Laugh with your spouse and your kids and your friends. Laugh often and long.

> A cheerful heart is good medicine, but a broken spirit saps a person's strength.
> PROVERBS 17:22

Love to Serve and Give

Maggie loves to have a job. She is happiest when she patrols the backyard and keeps the squirrels, birds, and bugs out of her kingdom. I really think she is convinced that she is conducting an important service for her pack by keeping the backyard secure and safe from intruders. The happiest people I know are those who serve and give their lives away. Giving your time to serve others is so counterintuitive to the self-centered messages that we are bombarded with every day. If I decided to live fully in the moment, I would prepare by spending a little time each day in Philippians 2, Colossians 3, and Romans 12. Here are some sample verses to get you started.

> Do everything without complaining and arguing, so that no one can criticize you. Live clean, innocent lives as children of God, shining like bright lights in a world full of crooked and perverse people.
>
> PHILIPPIANS 2:14-15

> Above all, clothe yourselves with love, which binds us all together in perfect harmony. And let the peace that comes from Christ rule in your hearts. For as members of one body you are called to live in peace. And always be thankful.
>
> COLOSSIANS 3:14-15

> Don't just pretend to love others. Really love them. Hate what is wrong. Hold tightly to what is good. Love each other with genuine affection, and take delight in honoring each other. Never be lazy, but work hard and serve the Lord enthusiastically. Rejoice in our confident hope. Be patient in trouble, and keep on praying. When

God's people are in need, be ready to help them. Always be eager to practice hospitality.

ROMANS 12:9-13

Love Grace

There was no better earthly example of grace than my friend Hannah. If grace is defined as unmerited or undeserved favor, then I would have nominated Hannah as the poster dog. But Hannah's grace was just an infinitesimal fraction of the grace God extended to me when I had nothing to offer Him except sin and brokenness. He willingly gave me His best when I offered only my worst. Nothing has changed my life more than beginning to understand the radical, mind-blowing extent of God's grace.

Grace allows me to quit *trying to be* righteous and actually *begin to be* righteous as I focus on the One who gave me the gift of grace. Grace allows me to deal with sin instead of trying to manage and rationalize it. Grace is real and powerful. It is not weak or cheap. If you think grace is cheap, go to the foot of the cross, look up, and see what grace price was paid for every person on earth. Grace should never be my cover for sin. Instead grace is my only hope to deal with it. Grace makes me tremble when I think of an almighty and powerful God who loved someone unlovable like me. Why would He give such a gift to an unworthy child? And how could I be comfortable taking advantage of that amazing grace? I cannot. I pray that I will not. Grace is compelling. I want it to be compelling in my life as well. Real grace works. Love grace with abandon.

God saved you by his grace when you believed. And you can't take credit for this; it is a gift from God.

EPHESIANS 2:8

Love Today

Hannah woke up convinced that every day was the best day ever. Maggie does the same. I think Satan's strategy is devastatingly simple and effective. He wants us to live in regret of the past and fear of the future, effectively robbing us of the joy of today. Find something to love each day, even on your worst day. Trust me; it's out there.

> The LORD is my strength and shield.
> I trust him with all my heart.
> He helps me, and my heart is filled
> with joy.
> PSALM 28:7

Love Learning

I have always heard that you cannot teach an old dog new tricks. Not true. We thought that Hannah only wanted to play with tennis balls for her first eight years. It never occurred to us to try anything different until we were traveling and left her in the care of a fellow dog lover who had plush toys. When we returned, we discovered that Hannah *loved* plush toys; we kept her supplied with a variety of them for the rest of her days. I had some bad teaching in my early journey with Jesus, but I have never stopped learning and pursuing the truth and what it means to be a disciple of Christ. Like Hannah did with her newfound playthings, I plan to enjoy His grace, identity, and freedom for the rest of my days.

> Intelligent people are always ready to learn.
> Their ears are open for knowledge.
> PROVERBS 18:15

Love Jesus

Hannah ran to her master whenever she was scared, confused, sad, or lonely. She just wanted to be at my side. I need to do the same with my Master.

Recently I talked to a friend of mine whose son returned from a youth mission trip to Costa Rica. When my friend asked his son about the trip, his answer was telling. "Dad, they aren't like Christians in America. They really love Jesus."

I know that many people really love Jesus in this country. But what the teenager saw in Costa Rica was unashamed, authentic, and complete devotion to Christ. Really loving Jesus is different from being content with the Savior. Jesus wants to be Lord in our lives as we grow in relationship with Him.

Believe, really believe, who you are in Christ. A forgiven person. A saint with no condemnation who is adored by God. Trust Jesus because He is trustworthy. I think that would be the best advice of all to live fully in the moment.

I don't know how much time I have left in my eternity warm-up act. It may be twenty minutes, twenty months, or twenty years. But if I use this passage from Colossians as a basic playbook, I will live well for whatever time God gives me.

> Christ is all that matters, and he lives in all of us.
>
> Since God chose you to be the holy people he loves, you must clothe yourselves with tenderhearted mercy, kindness, humility, gentleness, and patience. Make allowance for each other's faults, and forgive anyone who offends you. Remember, the Lord forgave you, so you must forgive others. Above all, clothe yourselves with love, which binds us all together in perfect harmony. And let the peace that comes from Christ

rule in your hearts. For as members of one body you are called to live in peace. And always be thankful.

Let the message about Christ, in all its richness, fill your lives. Teach and counsel each other with all the wisdom he gives. Sing psalms and hymns and spiritual songs to God with thankful hearts. And whatever you do or say, do it as a representative of the Lord Jesus, giving thanks through him to God the Father.

COLOSSIANS 3:11-17

My prayer for you is that you will always have the blessing of walking with a friend. Whether that friend has four or two legs, I pray you will enjoy this journey in the moment with someone at your side. But I also pray that you will remember that no matter what your circumstances might be, you always have a Friend. When you place your trust in Jesus, He walks by your side every step of every day. That's a promise you can count on.

Remember that there is joy to be found in every day. Maggie is illustrating this point even now. As I write this, she is chasing bugs around the pool with sheer delight.

If I can take a moment to count how blessed I am today, I can celebrate little things as well. There is joy even in the mundane events of life. There is sacredness in the routine. Ask the Spirit of God to show you that each day. As for me, I am going to take my spiritual mentor for a walk. I still have much to learn.

Afterword

MY NEW RESCUED MENTOR, Maggie, has continued to grow up. She now knows her name and understands that when I call her name nothing bad is going to happen.

She has stopped inappropriate chewing, counter surfing, and digging random holes in the backyard. She is becoming more affectionate and trusting. As you can see from this face, she is a very curious and sweet young lady.

It has been fun to see how patience, love, and grace-filled boundaries have helped her settle in with us. She is finding out how great a dip in the pool feels on a Texas summer day.

And Maggie has introduced her own unique talent—acrobatic bug chasing—to our family canine talent show. As soon as the dog agility competitions add a June Bug Chasing Championship, our Maggie will be the favorite in her weight class.

I have to admit that Hannah took a piece of my heart when she died, but there was still plenty of heart-room left for my new friend. Life continues and others need to be loved. To be honest, Maggie has been a challenge compared to Hannah. But that is how relationships of love go. Some are easier than others, but all are worth the effort.

The apostle Peter said it well in his first letter, words that we all should take to heart.

> Most important of all, continue to show deep love for each other, for love covers a multitude of sins.
>
> 1 PETER 4:8

We all fall short. We all sin. We all need love when we fail. We all need grace. My prayer for all of us is that we will become infectious carriers of God's amazing grace.

Acknowledgments

THIS PROJECT WOULD NOT HAVE HAPPENED without the affirmation and brotherhood of three men in my life. Thanks to Ed Underwood, Kevin Butcher, and Don Jacobson for encouraging me to keep writing through the self-esteem–rattling experience of publisher rejections. My life and walk with Jesus is much richer because of the honesty and grace I receive from these men.

Thanks to my agent, Don Jacobson, who believed in me when I didn't. Thanks to Blair Jacobson and the team at D.C. Jacobson & Associates for challenging me to think through every aspect of this project before it was pitched. I am convinced that process was a key component to publication.

Thanks to Jon Farrar and the acquisitions team at Tyndale House Publishers, who saw the potential in this unusual presentation of grace and faith. Thanks to my editor, Bonne Steffen, who makes me look like a lukewarm dog lover by comparison. Your loving investment in this book has made it far better, and I am grateful to you.

Thanks to my wonderful family, who put up with my "dad" jokes and embarrassing chatting up of strangers in public places. Much love to Matt and Holly, Scott and

Caroline, and Brett. Each one of you blesses me more than I can express.

Thanks to Joni, the love of my life. You stood by me through crazy schemes and ridiculous dreams. You believed in me when few did. You loved me when I was hard to love. You often parented solo when I was building a career. You clearly did an amazing job. You accepted and embraced my love for dogs. You endured three decades of muddy paws, chewed-up furniture, and dog hair flying through the air. You accepted that a house with three boys and a dog was not going to be a pristine model home. Your love created a home that nurtured all of us and gave us freedom. Your faith and strength through your own adversity inspired and changed me. God gave me the perfect partner when you inexplicably said yes. I love you.

In Memory

JUST A FEW WEEKS after the editing and revisions were completed on this book, Hannah's best friend, Sadie, finished her journey. She was a sweet and gentle spirit who graced our family with nearly fourteen years of loving faithfulness. Hannah would want her best friend to be remembered. You were loved as much as you loved Scott, Caroline, and "your" precious babies, Bennett and Clara. Good-bye, Miss Sadie.

Notes

BE PRESENT

1. Deborah M. Custance and Jennifer Mayer, "Empathic-Like Responding by Domestic Dogs (Canis Familiaris) to Distress in Humans: An Exploratory Study," *Animal Cognition* 15 (May 2012): 851–859.
2. Henri J. M. Nouwen, *Out of Solitude: Three Meditations on the Christian Life*, rev. ed. (Notre Dame, IN: Ave Maria Press, 2004), 38.

LIVE IN THE MOMENT

1. C. S. Lewis, *Christian Reflections* (Grand Rapids, MI: William B. Eerdmans, 1967), 113.

GOOD FRIENDS

1. Anne Lamott, *Bird by Bird* (New York: Anchor Books, 1995), 22.
2. Howard Hendricks, "Paul, Barnabas, and Timothy," in *Men of Integrity: A Daily Guide to the Bible and Prayer*, ed. Harry Genet, Ashley Nearn, and Linda Gehrs (Nashville, TN: Word Publishing, 1999), 16.
3. Joshua Wolf Shenk, "What Makes Us Happy?" *The Atlantic*, June 1, 2009, http://www.theatlantic.com/magazine/archive/2009/06/what-makes-us-happy/307439/2/?single_page=true.

RUN TO THE MASTER

1. Quoted in Nick Lannon, "Things Fall Apart . . . for RGIII," *Liberate* (blog), August 26, 2013, http://liberate.org/2013/08/26/things-fall-apart-for-rgiii/.
2. Timothy Keller, *Walking with God through Pain and Suffering* (New York: Dutton, 2013), 234.

SHAKE OFF THE LIES

1. Enjoy this article on the very same topic: Alexis C. Madrigal, "Science: Dogs Can Shake 70% of the Water from Their Fur in 4 Seconds, Here's How," *The Atlantic*, August 15, 2012, http://www.theatlantic.com/technology/archive/2012/08/science-dogs-can-shake-70-of-the-water-from-their-fur-in-4-seconds-heres-how/261191.
2. Timothy Keller, *Every Good Endeavor: Connecting Your Work to God's Work* (New York: Dutton, 2012), 137.

LIVE OUT OF WHO YOU ARE

1. Watch Andrew Peterson, Ben Shive, and Andy Gullahorn perform this song at http://www.youtube.com/watch?v=o0SBamE107Y.
2. Henri J. M. Nouwen, *Bread for the Journey: A Daybook of Wisdom and Faith* (New York: HarperCollins, 1997), April 23.
3. Truefaced is an invaluable resource for helping people experience this reformation of God's grace by restoring the lost blueprint of trusting and loving. The "Two Roads, Two Rooms" message challenged and completely changed my thinking about grace. See http://www.youtube.com/watch?v=Rfy03PEVUhQ.
4. John Lynch, Bruce McNicol, and Bill Thrall, *The Cure* (Colorado Springs, CO: NavPress, 2011), 29.
5. C. S. Lewis, *The Four Loves* (San Diego, CA: Harcourt Brace Jovanovich, 1960), 96–97.

GRATITUDE STARTS WITH ATTITUDE

1. George Herbert, *Poems* (New York: Alfred A. Knopf, 2004), 148.
2. Ed Underwood, *When God Breaks Your Heart: Choosing Hope in the Midst of Faith-Shattering Circumstances* (Colorado Springs, CO: David C. Cook, 2008), 58.
3. C. S. Lewis, *The Collected Letters of C. S. Lewis: Books, Broadcasts, and the War 1939–1949*, ed. Walter Hooper (New York: Harper Collins, 2004), 869.
4. Philip Yancey, *What's So Amazing about Grace?* (Grand Rapids, MI: Zondervan, 1997), 112.

BURY THE BONES OF BITTERNESS

1. Bill Thrall, Bruce McNicol, and John Lynch, *TrueFaced Experience Edition* (Colorado Springs, CO: NavPress, 2004).
2. Marilyn Elias, "Psychologists Now Know What Makes People Happy," *USA Today*, December 8, 2002, http://usatoday30.usatoday.com/news/health/2002-12-08-happy-main_x.htm.
3. Quoted in Tullian Tchividjian, *One Way Love* (Colorado Springs, CO: Cook Publishing, 2013), 72.

WELCOME WAGGIN'

1. Quoted in *Humour for All Ages*, ed. Mel Bergstresser (Bloomington, IN: Xlibris LLC, 2013), 83.
2. Dave Barry, "Earning a Collie Degree," *Miami Herald*, September 8, 1985, http://www.miamiherald.com/2011/07/31/2279225/earning-a-collie-degree.html.
3. Karen Allen, Jim Blascovich, and Wendy B. Mendes, "Cardiovascular Reactivity and the Presence of Pets, Friends, and Spouses: The Truth About Cats and Dogs," *Psychosomatic Medicine* 64, no. 5 (September/October 2002): 727–739.

ONLY THE GOOD DIE YOUNG?

1. Sir Walter Scott, *The Complete Works of Sir Walter Scott with a Biography and His Last Additions and Illustrations in Seven Volumes—Vol. VII* (New York: Conner & Cooke, 1833), 371.
2. Dan Patrick, *SportsCenter*, IMDb.com, http://www.imdb.com/title/tt0136668/quotes.
3. See John 14:1-3.
4. Dietrich Bonhoeffer, quoted by Eric Metaxas in *Bonhoeffer: Pastor, Martyr, Prophet, Spy* (Nashville, TN: Thomas Nelson, 2010), 531.
5. Randy Alcorn, *The Treasure Principle: Discovering the Secret of Joyful Giving* (Colorado Springs, CO: Multnomah Books, 2001), 42.
6. C. S. Lewis, *Mere Christianity* (San Francisco: HarperSanFrancisco, 2009), 136–137.
7. See this happy reunion at http://www.youtube.com/watch?v=SAbCyA2rbxM.

GOOD-BYE

1. Billy Graham, "Will There Be Animals in Heaven?" ArcaMax, January 30, 2013, http://www.arcamax.com/religionandspirituality/billygraham/s-1260302.
2. George Graham Vest, "Tribute to the Dog," *The History Place*, http://www.historyplace.com/speeches/vest.htm. The recording of "Tribute to a Dog" by Walter Brennan is found on the album *Old Shep* © 2000 Universal Special Products.

THE IMPACT OF OUR STORY

1. See Romans 5:6-8.
2. See Luke 15:11-24.
3. See Luke 15:25-32.
4. See Matthew 20:1-16.
5. See Romans 8:14-16.
6. See Romans 5:10-11.
7. See Ephesians 2:13.
8. See Colossians 3:10.
9. David Kinnaman, *UnChristian* (Grand Rapids, MI: Baker, 2007), 28, 182.
10. See Romans 8:1-2.
11. Russell D. Moore, "A Purpose-Driven Cosmos: Why Jesus Doesn't Promise Us an 'Afterlife,'" *Christianity Today*, February 27, 2012, http://www.christianitytoday.com/ct/2012/february/jesus-afterlife.html?paging=off.
12. Henri J. M. Nouwen, *Here and Now: Living in the Spirit* (New York: Crossroad Publishing, 2006), 71.

SIT! STAY!

1. Dane Ortlund, *Defiant Grace: The Surprising Message and Mission of Jesus* (Faverdale North, Darlington, England: Evangelical Press, 2011).

GENTLY LEADING

1. James Botts, "Rest for the Stressed" (sermon, The Crossing Community Church, Crystal Lake, IL, August 11, 2002), http://www.sermoncentral .com/sermons/rest-for-the-stressed-james-botts-sermon-on-fulfillment -49844.asp.

2. Tullian Tchividjian, Twitter post, February 9, 2013, 4:08 p.m., https:// twitter.com/PastorTullian/status/300380784072720385.

3. Justin Martyr, *Justin Martyr's Dialogue with Trypho the Jew*, ed. Henry Brown (Oxford: W. Jackson, 1745), 65.

LIFE INTERRUPTED

1. I heard this on a podcast while I was walking, from Tullian Tchividjian's book *Surprised by Grace: God's Relentless Pursuit of Rebels* (Wheaton, IL: Crossway Books, 2010), 57–58.

2. Paul Tautges, "The Difference between Punishment and Discipline," *Counseling One Another* (blog), October 14, 2013, http://counseling oneanother.com/2013/10/14/the-difference-between-punishment -and-discipline/.

3. This heading is in the New Living Translation, Second Edition, published in 2004. In the *NLT Study Bible*, the heading was changed to "Endure by Keeping Your Eyes on Jesus" for Hebrews 12:1-4, followed by the heading "Endure God's Loving Discipline" for Hebrews 12:5-13.

4. Jerry Bridges, *The Discipline of Grace: God's Role and Our Role in the Pursuit of Holiness* (Colorado Springs, CO: NavPress, 2006), 93.

O MAGGIE, WHERE ART THOU?

1. Tim Keller Wisdom, Twitter post, September 5, 2013, 2:08 p.m., https:// twitter.com/DailyKeller/status/375727076587741184.

2. *The Onion*, "Report: Today [*sic*] the Day They Find Out You're a Fraud," January 31, 2014, http://www.theonion.com/articles/report-today-the -day-they-find-out-youre-a-fraud,35133/.

LEARNING TO LIVE

1. Cesar Millan, "What Your Pet Can Teach You," *Parade*, January 11, 2009, http://parade.condenast.com/39524/parade/what-your-pet-can-teach-you/.

2. Ibid.

About the Author

DAVE BURCHETT has been a successful television sports director for more than thirty years. His experiences have included the Olympic Games as well as professional and collegiate sports. He has collected a national Emmy and two local Emmys over his career.

When the writing bug bit Dave more than a decade ago, he would have never guessed that a book about his dogs would be his favorite project. His first published book was the well-received *When Bad Christians Happen to Good People*, followed by the acclaimed book on church healing, *Bring 'Em Back Alive*, and most recently *Waking Up Slowly* and *Between the White Lines*.

Dave has developed a speaking ministry as well as a popular blog on his website, daveburchett.com.

His heart is for people who have been wounded by the church and by life. As he was praying for a way to communicate the message of grace in a unique and winsome way, his Labrador retriever, Hannah, was diagnosed with cancer. He began journaling his feelings and reactions to her impending death. Reluctantly, Dave shared some of the material with friends, and they affirmed the power of the message he was learning from this unique relationship. His prayer is that God can use this message to give hope to people facing disappointment, trials, and loss.

Dave and his wife, Joni, have three grown sons, six grandchildren, and another rescued Lab named Maggie.

The heartwarming true tale of an irrepressible donkey who needed a home —and forever changed a family.

RACHEL ANNE RIDGE

The Homeless Donkey Who Taught Me about Life, Faith, and Second Chances

Foreword by Priscilla Shirer

Flash

978-1-4143-9783-2

When Rachel Anne Ridge discovered a wounded, frightened donkey standing in her driveway, she couldn't turn him away. And against all odds, he turned out to be the very thing her family needed most. They let him into their hearts . . . and he taught them things they never knew about life, love, and faith.

Prepare to fall in love with Flash: a quirky, unlikely hero with gigantic ears, a deafening bray, a personality as big as Texas, and a story you'll never forget.

Available everywhere books are sold

CP0850